For That
Most Wonderful Day . . .

This thoroughly practical and thorough guide offers the bridal couple a truly unique opportunity to create their own wedding with ease and grace, and even answers the sensitive questions that other manuals dismiss or neglect:

- Are the parents of the couple divorced or remarried?
- Is this not the first trip to the altar for bride or groom?
- What type of wedding is appropriate when a bride of moderate means marries a wealthy man?
- Who pays for what?

In short, here are the answers to the expected—and unexpected—questions that occur, answers that will make a glorious occasion of that most wonderful day!

Your
Wedding
HOW TO
PLAN AND ENJOY IT

Marjorie Binford Woods

ILLUSTRATIONS BY VASILIU

Newly Revised and Updated

A JOVE BOOK

YOUR WEDDING:
How to Plan and Enjoy It

A Jove Book / published by arrangement with
the author

PRINTING HISTORY
Seven previous paperback printings
Jove edition / September 1977
Twelfth printing / June 1986

ISBN: 0-515-08543-X

Jove Books are published by The Berkley Publishing Group,
200 Madison Avenue, New York, N.Y. 10016.
The words "A JOVE BOOK" and the "J" with sunburst
are trademarks belonging to Jove Publications, Inc.

PRINTED IN THE UNITED STATES OF AMERICA

Contents

INTRODUCTION: *FROM THIS DAY FORTH* 11

CHAPTER 1: *A TOKEN AND PLEDGE* 13
How Shall I Announce My Engagement? 13
    Special Situations 14
How About an Announcement Party? 16
Prenuptial Parties 17
    Who Should Give Showers? 17
    Kinds of Showers 17
    Entertaining for Your Bridesmaids 18
    Will there be a Bachelor Dinner? 18
    The Bridal Dinner 19
    The Meeting of the Clan 20

CHAPTER 2: *RULES TO HONOUR AND OBEY* 21
The Bride's Working Schedule 22
    Check List for Pre-wedding Week 24
What Type of Wedding for You? 26
    Responsibilities of the Bride's Family 27
    The Bride's Personal Responsibilities 28
    Responsibilities of the Bridegroom
    and His Family 28
Get Your Calendar In Hand 30
    What Hour for the Wedding? 30
    What Sort of Reception Should Follow? 31
Special Tips to Members of Both Families 31
    The Bride's Family 31
    Mother's Responsibilities 32
    Dear Old Dad 33
    The Groom's Family 33
    Reminders for the Groom 35

CHAPTER 3: *CHOOSING YOUR WEDDING PLAN* 38
  WILL IT BE A FORMAL CHURCH WEDDING? 38
    Arrival at the Church 42
    Preliminaries to the Ceremony 44
    Procedure for Leaving the Church 45
  THE FORMAL HOME WEDDING 45
    Keep a Home Atmosphere 46
    Processional and Recessional 48
  THE CLUB OR HOTEL WEDDING 48
  WHAT TO WEAR FOR A FORMAL DAYTIME WEDDING ...49
  WHAT TO WEAR FOR A FORMAL EVENING WEDDING ...50
  THE SEMIFORMAL WEDDING 51
  WHAT TO WEAR FOR A SEMIFORMAL
    DAYTIME WEDDING 52
  WHAT TO WEAR FOR A SEMIFORMAL
    EVENING WEDDING 53
  THE INFORMAL WEDDING 54
  WHAT TO WEAR FOR AN INFORMAL DAYTIME
    OR EVENING WEDDING...................56
  THE MILITARY WEDDING 57
    Military Protocol Reminders 58
    Military Dress Regulations 59
  THE GARDEN WEDDING 59
  THE DOUBLE WEDDING 61
  IF IT IS ALTAR TRIP NUMBER TWO..........61
  THE OLDER BRIDE 62
  THE CIVIL CEREMONY 63
  SPECIAL QUESTIONS AND ANSWERS 63
    What Kind of Wedding Is Appropriate? 63

CHAPTER 4: *THE HONOUR OF YOUR
  PRESENCE IS REQUESTED*...................66
  MAKING UP YOUR LISTS 67
  WHO ISSUES THE INVITATIONS?............67
  FORM OF INVITATION.....................68
    Wording of Invitation 69
    Reception Cards 70
    Typical Invitation Forms 70
    Invitations Keyed to Special Situations 74
    Double Weddings 79
    Military Weddings 80
  ANNOUNCEMENTS 82
    Special Announcements 83
  ADDRESSING INVITATIONS OR ANNOUNCEMENTS 84
    Return Address 87
    Special Courtesies. 87
  WHEN TO MAIL..........................87
  WHEN WEDDING INVITATIONS MUST BE RECALLED ...88

CHAPTER 5: *IN THE PRESENCE OF THIS COMPANY* 89
   How Many Bridesmaids? 90
   Maid and Matron of Honor 90
   Junior Bridesmaids 91
   Flower Girls 92
   Ring Bearer 92
   General Responsibilities of the Bride's Attendants 93
   Ushers 93
   Who Is to Give You Away? 94
   The Best Man 95

CHAPTER 6: *IN HOLY WEDLOCK* 97
   Church Regulations 98
   Nuances in Wedding Ceremonies 99
   Church Fees 99
   The Marriage Ceremony 100

CHAPTER 7: *TO BE REMEMBERED AS LONG AS YOU BOTH SHALL LIVE* 101
   Choosing Your Wedding Gown 102
     Wedding Gown Colors and Fabrics 103
     Harmony Is the Thing 105
     What Length Train? 105
     To Preserve Your Wedding Gown 106
   Your Wedding Veil 106
   What Color Hose? 108
   Wedding Shoes 109
   Will You Need Gloves? 109
   Your Complete Wedding Outfit 109
   It's Time To Outfit Your Attendants! 110
     Fabrics 113
     Headdresses 114
     Gloves and Shoes 114
   The Mothers' Costumes 115
     For Daytime Formal Weddings 116
     For Evening Formal Weddings 117

CHAPTER 8: *ROSE PETALS IN YOUR PATHWAY* 118
   Church Decorations 119
     For a Springtime Wedding 121
     Is It to Be a Summertime Ceremony? 121
     For an Autumn Wedding 123
     A Winter Wedding 124
   Flowers for a Home Wedding 124
   A Garden Wedding 125
   Flowers for the Reception Tables 126
   Your Bridal Bouquet 128

Corsages for Informal Weddings 128
Bridesmaids' Bouquets 129

CHAPTER 9: *TO LOVE AND TO TREASURE*.......131
Linens 132
Your Bedroom Linens........................132
Blankets 133
Minimum Requirements for Bed Linens 134
Bathroom Linens 134
Kitchen Linens 135
Table Linens 136
Selecting Your Dinnerware 137
Fine China, Earthenware and Pottery 137
Molded Plastic Dinnerware 139
Deciding Factors 139
Minimum Requirements for China 140
Selecting Your Silver 141
What Type of Pattern for You? 142
How Much to Buy 144
Silver Plate 145
Other Flatware 146
Suggested List for Holloware 147
Monograms 147
Choosing Your Glassware 148
Decoration of Glassware 150
How to Judge Good Glass 150
How Much to Buy 151
Other Selections in Glass 152

CHAPTER 10: *TO HAVE AND TO HOLD* 154
Displaying Your Gifts 155
Writing Your Thank-You Notes 156
When a Gift Has to Be Returned 158
Special Questions and Answers 159
For Your Attendants 159
From the Bridegroom to His Attendants 160
When to Present the Attendants' Gifts 160
Gifts to Other Friends Who Serve
at Your Wedding 160
From the Bride to the Groom 161

CHAPTER 11: *STRAINS OF LOHENGRIN* 162
Preliminary Music 162
Are You Having a Vocalist? 163
Preliminary Music for Home Wedding 165
Music for the Processional and Recessional 165
During the Ceremony 166
Reception Music 166

CHAPTER 12: *MEMORIES TO CHERISH* 167
   THE RECEIVING LINE 168
   PLANNING THE DETAILS OF THE RECEPTION 169
   A WEDDING BREAKFAST OR SUPPER 171
   THE AFTERNOON WEDDING 171
   THE BRIDE'S CAKE 171
      Cutting the Cake .172
   BRIDAL-TABLE SEATING ARRANGEMENTS 173
   WHAT TO DRINK? 174
   A TOAST TO THE BRIDE 175
   DANCING PROCEDURE. 176
   A BORROWED EUROPEAN CUSTOM. 177
   MENU SUGGESTIONS 178
      Sit-Down Breakfast Suggestions 179
      Buffet Breakfast .179
      Afternoon Reception. 179
      Evening Supper 180
   TOSSING YOUR BOUQUET 180
   SAYING YOUR FAREWELLS 180
   CHECK LIST FOR ANY RECEPTION 181

CHAPTER 13: *RECORDING THE PROCEEDINGS* . . .183
   TYPICAL WEDDING ANNOUNCEMENT 184
   YOUR WEDDING PHOTOGRAPHS 186

CHAPTER 14: *PROCEDURE FOR GUESTS.* 188
   YOU ARE INVITED TO A WEDDING 188
   TYPICAL FORMAL ACCEPTANCE 189
   TYPICAL FORMAL REPLY SENDING REGRETS 189
   REPLIES TO INFORMAL INVITATIONS 190
   UPON RECEIPT OF A WEDDING ANNOUNCEMENT 190
   IT'S TIME TO SEND A WEDDING GIFT 191
   SHOWER GIFTS 192
   CHURCH WEDDINGS 192
   GUEST INFORMATION FOR A HOME OR CLUB
     WEDDING. 193
   RECEIVING-LINE PROCEDURE 193
   DINING-ROOM ETIQUETTE 194
   SPECIAL NICETIES 194

CHAPTER 15: *FOR BETTER OR FOR WORSE.* 196
   WHO IS TO TAKE CHARGE?. 196
   WHO SHOULD ATTEND THE WEDDING REHEARSAL?. . . .197
   CORRECT PROCEDURE TO THE ALTAR 197
   AT THE ALTAR 200
   THE RECESSIONAL 200
   INSTRUCTIONS TO THE USHERS 201
   REMINDERS FOR THE BEST MAN 204
   MAID OF HONOR 204

CHAPTER 16: *"I PLEDGE THEE MY TROTH"* 206

INTRODUCTION | From This Day Forth

Dear Bride-to-be:

The little book you are holding in your hand has been especially designed for you, the bride of today. It offers you all the keys for having an easy and happy time planning *your* wedding, without a lot of fuss and feathers.

Whether you have an informal home ceremony or a big church wedding, you can write your own ticket (with due consideration for Dad's bank account), and use as much originality as you choose. Your plans will fall easily into place if you carry them out with all attention to good manners, tradition and convenience.

If a large formal affair is not feasible, an intimate at-home ceremony with relatives and best friends gathered around could be most heart-warming and delightful. It has been proved on many occasions that some of the most beautiful weddings have been the most unpretentious and unfettered in their planning.

It isn't so much the effect that a beautiful wedding will present to your guests that makes it worth all the

11

doing. Most important is what it does for you and your bridegroom. When your hearts are truly in the planning of this event—*your* wedding—with all its religious solemnity and atmosphere of beauty, it builds a bond of love and promise that cannot easily be put asunder.

So, put your mind and heart into this momentous happening and keep singing your way along.

Don't forget the bridegroom, as you find yourself knee-deep in shopping, shower parties and wedding plans. It is *his* wedding too, remember, and he should have a say-so all along the way. The more he knows about what is going on, the less bewildered he will be, and the more help he can provide.

Do try to maintain a gay and loving attitude through your busy days, even when the little nettles seem to come. Hold fast to the beauty of all the romantic moments . . . the fun of assembling your bridesmaids for their dress fittings. The day you and your beloved set forth to the Marriage License Bureau to make your dreams come true . . . the thrill of choosing your wedding rings together, and then celebrating the occasion with a rapturous tête-è-tête luncheon.

Then there's the exciting arrival of your first wedding gifts. (It will be an added thrill if you wait and open them together.)

There is bound to be a round of parties in honor of you two, and showers and showers of blessedness. Just think . . . all of this to be followed by the wonder of *your wedding* itself, thrilling and beautiful . . . because you have made it so.

A wedding to be remembered as long as you both shall live.

Do have a happy, happy time.

Marjorie Binford Woods

CHAPTER 1 | A Token and Pledge

HOW SHALL I ANNOUNCE MY ENGAGEMENT?

Don't depend on the grapevine route and don't send out engraved announcements.

Scatter the tidings by note to close friends and relatives. Then tell the rest of the world of your engagement by formal announcement in local newspapers, both yours and the bridegroom's. The simple way of proclaiming the news is the smartest way.

Your family should sponsor this announcement, and the task of sending the information to the society editors falls to your mother. The item should be a mere statement of fact, typed in double space, with release date clearly marked and your telephone number listed for verification. The customary deadline for Sunday editions is early in the week, so be sure to check if you wish a weekend announcement.

Order glossy prints from the photographic studio if your picture is to appear with the notice. Mark name and address on back of photos for identification.

You may make your announcement three or four months before the wedding and withhold the wedding date until later. Or you may want to announce a definite wedding date if one has been set.

Your friends will appreciate it more if they have a breathing spell for planning prenuptial parties. It will also give you a leisurely period for spinning your marriage plans—and a definite date to work toward.

Don't announce your engagement further ahead than a year or less than six weeks before the wedding date.

As a guide for your announcement notice to the papers, follow one of these forms:

Mr. and Mrs. William Graham Brown announce the engagement of their daughter, Nancy Ann, to Mr. Paul Allen Tucker, son of Mr. and Mrs. George Marvin Tucker. No date has been set for the wedding.

Or:

The engagement has been announced of Miss Nancy Ann Brown, daughter of Mr. and Mrs. William Graham Brown, to Mr. Paul Allen Tucker, son of Mr. and Mrs. George Marvin Tucker. The wedding will take place in the spring.

Or you may announce the definite time and place of the wedding in either form. If the society editors wish more details in the announcement, you may include facts on schooling and club memberships, along with information on your fiancé's business affiliation.

When in doubt, be as brief as possible and model your announcement after those used in your own community papers.

Any Questions?

Q. How should the engagement be announced when the bride's parents are divorced?

A. When the bride-to-be is living with her divorced mother, the announcement is made in the mother's name. If her mother has married again, she may, if everyone desires, send out the announcement in the name of the stepfather as well. It may read:

"Mr. and Mrs. Clifford Berg announce the engagement of her daughter, Mary Stewart White, to . . ."

The same rule applies if the girl makes her home with her father and he is acting as sponsor for the wedding, even though her mother is still living.

It is not considered good taste for divorced parents to sponsor together their daughter's wedding.

Q. Is it necessary for the prospective groom to ask the girl's father for her hand, as formerly?

A. It's much more likely that these days a young couple will go together to the bride's family to break the news casually. However a serious talk between father and future son-in-law should take place soon.

Q. What is the bridegroom's parents' duty toward the bride at the time of the engagement?

A. The bride-elect naturally expects to be welcomed by her future in-laws. And it is their rightful duty to make the first gesture of acknowledgment to the bride and her family when the news becomes known to them. They either telephone immediately or call on them to express their pleasure over the engagement, and then make plans for entertaining their future daughter-in-law and her family with a tea, buffet supper or a get-together of some sort.

If the families live at a distance, the groom's mother will want to write at once to extend felicitations, and to invite the bride-to-be for a visit. If the young man's parents are not living, it is usual for his sister, aunt, grandmother, or nearest relative to respond to the announcement by writing, telephoning or entertaining both the bride and her family.

Q. What is the procedure when an engagement is broken?

A. If the engagement has been formally announced

in the papers, a notice should be sent immediately to the same papers. The notice usually takes this form:

The engagement of Miss Nancy Ann Brown and Mr. Paul Allen Tucker has been terminated by mutual consent.

The engagement ring and all presents should be returned at once. If wedding invitations have been issued, engraved cards should be sent to everyone who has received an invitation. If there is not sufficient time for engraved cards, members of the bride's family may recall the invitations verbally, by personal note, telegram or telephone.

In the tragic instance of a fiancé's death prior to the wedding, presents are always returned by thoughtful members of the bride's family.

HOW ABOUT AN ANNOUNCEMENT PARTY?

The party is your family's responsibility, although a close friend of the bride might want to do the honors. It could be a tea or luncheon just for the girls, with your mother as hostess. Do be sure to invite your prospective mother-in-law.

Or if you want something more gala, why not a cocktail party or a dance? Actually, elaborate announcement parties are in the minority it seems.

The simplest type of announcement would be place cards at a luncheon or dinner party—in the form of a newspaper clipping proclaiming your news. For an attractive centerpiece, you might make an arrangement of dainty flowers centered with appealing boy-and-girl figurines.

Make it a very festive occasion, but don't overdo the cupid theme!

Pre-wedding Parties

Of course you'll have a great time entertaining your bridal party and other friends who stop in to see your wedding gifts. It's delightful to have lots of showers and other fun doings, but too many festive events can wear everyone out, including you.

After each shower, be sure to send a thank-you note to your hostess and personal notes to all gift-givers.

Who Should Give Showers?

Your best friends naturally, but the bridegroom's immediate family or yours should never give showers.

Kinds of Showers

The setting for a shower may be almost anything—a breakfast, luncheon, dinner or afternoon tea for "ladies only." Or it may be a cocktail party, dance, supper or evening party where the bridegroom and his friends are included.

If you are asked to specify the kinds of showers you would like, you may mention with perfect propriety any of your personal choices. They may include anything from linen, kitchen, bar and bathroom showers, to boudoir, notions or cupboard delicacies.

An "idea shower" is a novelty with no drain on the pocketbook. The hostess provides a leather-bound loose-leaf notebook with the bride's name inscribed on the cover. The guests then contribute to the book by filling the pages with favorite household tricks, coveted recipes and helpful ideas to start her on the right track as a homemaker.

There are book showers and magazine subscription showers appropriate for couples who are avid readers, or a library shower.

A wine or liqueur shower for both bride and groom

might be appreciated if your fiancé wishes to stock up for later entertaining.

Shower invitations may be issued by informally written notes or by telephone, telegram or by novelty invitations devised by a clever hostess.

Joint showers for both bride and groom are popular with many couples. In these instances, the gifts should be of the household type, rather than items of a personal nature.

Your mother and the bridegroom's mother are often invited to your shower parties, but as honor guests they are not asked to contribute to the shower fund or to bring individual gifts.

Entertaining for Your Bridesmaids

A farewell luncheon for your bridal party is a traditional part of the festivities of a big formal wedding. It is sometimes called "the spinster luncheon" (or dinner) and should take place a few days before the wedding. You may give your presents to the attendants at this party if you wish, or you may present them at the bridal dinner, or at an informal ceremony at your home.

Invitations usually are issued by word of mouth or by an informal note, and the occasion may be as festive in décor as you want to make it. Often there's a bride's cake with pink icing and sentimental fortunes for everyone.

This party may be given even though the wedding is not to be formal. Or you may entertain your attendants more simply at an afternoon tea or trousseau affair where they can have a look at your new wardrobe.

Is There To Be a Bachelor Dinner?

The groom has a perfect right to round up his friends and attendants for a farewell party, too, if he wishes. Many bridegrooms omit the bachelor dinner nowadays because of the added expense, but it's a personal matter.

The dinner usually takes place at a club or in the private dining room of a hotel. Music is often provided, the guests invited informally by the groom, and the gifts to the ushers and best man presented at their places at table.

Though tradition has it that this dinner is a veritable carousal, this is rarely the case today. It is wise, however, to schedule the dinner to take place several nights before the wedding, so that there may be more free time for the bride and groom as the wedding nears.

According to custom, the age-honored glass-breaking ceremony is the high light of the bachelor dinner. In this sentimental rite the bridegroom, toward the end of the dinner, rises and holds his champagne-filled glass high as he says, "To the bride!" Every man rises, drinks the toast standing, then breaks the delicate stem of the wine glass. The idea of so destroying the glasses is that these particular wine glasses may never be used for "a less honorable purpose."

The Bridal Dinner

The bridal dinner (or rehearsal dinner, as it is often called) traditionally is given by the bride's family, but the groom's family may graciously take it over if they wish to do so.

The dinner may be given immediately following the rehearsal or preceding it. The invitation list includes the bride and groom, all members of the wedding party, their husbands and wives, the parents of the bride and groom, the clergyman and his wife (if they are well known to the host and hostess), the musicians (if they are personal friends), and any out-of-town relatives of the bridal pair who have come on for the wedding.

If the occasion is to be formal, it should be in the nature of a dinner with floral decorations and place cards (*see* bridal table chart for seating arrangements, page 173. If the wedding is less formal, it may be a buffet dinner or an after-rehearsal supper party.

Guests are invited by the hostess (either the bride's

mother or the groom's mother) for any type of bridal dinner. The invitations may be word of mouth or by personal note or by visiting card with time and place indicated. It is well to make sure at any party given during the wedding festivities that a beverage for toasting the bridal couple is provided—either alcoholic or nonalcoholic.

The dinner may be held in the family home, at a club, hotel or restaurant; and it is often on this occasion that the attendants' gifts are given by both the bride and the groom and are appropriately placed at each table setting.

The Meeting of the Clan

Sometime before the wedding the thoughtful bride will want to arrange an occasion at which uncles, aunts, cousins, grandparents and old friends of both families have an opportunity to meet and get acquainted. A Sunday afternoon tea or Sunday night supper would be appropriate, perhaps, and it should be a jolly, informal affair.

CHAPTER 2 | Rules to Honour and Obey

"How much time should I have to plan my wedding?" Everyone asks this question. The answer is up to you and your calendar.

Many a lovely wedding has been planned and carried out in a few short weeks without causing nervous collapse or family bankruptcy. So it *can* be done if you're geared for speed.

But actually it's like the great oaks and little acorns adage. You'll enjoy it more if you can start with the little things and give them time to grow. It will add to your resources and subtract from your liabilities in the long run.

You'll have more time to shop and so avoid the disappointment of hasty selections. You can be more deliberate in your plans and so have fewer mistakes to charge up to inexperience. Remember, too, that perfection of detail and the happy air of ease really come from careful preparation and advance concentration.

If your family is new at wedding preparations, you'll

all welcome a bride's time schedule to keep you moving steadily in the right direction.

Begin planning three months ahead if possible, and build a framework of budgets to cover "Wedding Expenses," "Reception Expenses," "Trousseau Expenses." Then add another budget for "Extras."

Fortify yourself with a notebook. Sharpen your pencil and follow the schedule step by step, noting down your decisions and checking off the things accomplished. This list is your working guide, and should be used constantly to check on your progress.

We recommend that you make each decision in the order in which the steps are presented here. Study each chapter to which you are referred and choose your own plan. Then go on to the next step.

To give you a graphic idea . . . here's the way to work.

Are you ready to decide on the type of wedding you'll have? Then turn to page 26 and study up on the various kinds of weddings there are. Get all the wise family heads together to assist with that big decision. Then set your date. *Now turn back to the Bride's Working Schedule* and check that off as settled. *Proceed to the next reminder and follow through in the same way, right up to the very last day.*

Of course you'll probably want to read through this book first. But after you have reviewed the whole job of wedding preparation and initial home planning, calm down and go at the schedule week by week. That's the purpose of it—to keep you steadily moving on a well-organized plan.

THE BRIDE'S WORKING SCHEDULE

First of all

Go into a family huddle and decide on:

    Type of wedding (page 38): Formal, Semiformal, Informal, Military, etc.

    Date and time (page 30).

Minister and organist. (Engage them now; the final date and time of your wedding depends on them. You'll see them later for a conference.)

Type of reception, breakfast, or what have you. (Get estimates on catering and music.)

Confer with your bridal counselor.

Choose your bridal attendants:

Your maid of honor, bridesmaids, flower girls, etc. (pages 90-96).

The bridegroom's best man (page 95) and ushers (page 93).

Next in order

Begin shopping for trousseau, linens and household items. Complete your guest lists and order:

Wedding invitations (page 66).

Announcements (page 85).

Notepaper for handwritten notes if it's an informal or semiformal wedding (page 68).

Thank-you paper (page 68).

Start addressing wedding invitations (page 84).

It's time to tell your friends your chosen patterns, after registering them at your favorite stores.

Shop for:

Wedding gown, veil, etc. (pages 101-110).

Bridesmaids' costumes (pages 110-115).

Your mothers' gown (pages 115-117).

Continue trousseau and household shopping.

Decide on gifts for your attendants (page 159).

Confer with florist and order flowers (pages 118-129).

Special reminders

Mail formal wedding invitations three weeks from the date. If invitations are to be handwritten, mail them two or three weeks ahead.

Have wedding-gown fittings and bridesmaids' fittings. *(Get samples of all dress materials.)*

Decide on musical selections for wedding (pages 162–166).

Arrange for display of gifts (page 155).

Acknowledge each gift the day it arrives (page 156).

Have your hair styled and get a permanent, if necessary.

Complete reception arrangements (pages 169-173).

Order the bride's cake and wedding-cake boxes if you are having them (page 171).

Arrange for photographer to take wedding pictures.

Gather material for newspaper story of wedding (page 184).

Have bridal photograph taken at last wedding-gown fitting.

Study rehearsal procedure for best altar effects (pages 196-205).

Arrange for either:

> Bridesmaids' luncheon four or five days before the wedding (page 18).

> Or bridal dinner before or after rehearsal the night before the wedding (page 19).

Make plans for billeting out-of-town guests.

See proofs of your wedding pictures. Order glossy prints for the newspapers.

If it's a formal wedding, decide whether to dress at home or at the church. Arrange for your bridal consultant or someone else to help you dress and start you down the aisle.

Have your medical examination, to meet required tests for marriage license.

Check List for Pre-wedding Week

6 days before:

> Check to see if all trousseau purchases have arrived.
>
> Right sizes? Any additions?
>
> Keep up to date with your thank-you notes.
>
> Eat regularly all week.
>
> Rest between times when you aren't receiving gifts

and the many friends who are sure to be dropping in from now on.

Appoint a *chargé d'affaires* (not a member of your immediate family) who will attend the last-minute details, receive wires, expedite serving at reception, etc.

5 *days before:*

Are you having a bridesmaids' luncheon? Everything ready? Better have someone dependable around all the time with a car to run errands.

Remember your note-writing.

Check and double check delivery instructions for all wedding clothes.

Confirm the wedding date with caterer, florist, etc.

4 *days before:*

Do you have your wedding pictures?

Have ready all the wedding information for the newspapers.

Are the gifts rolling in? Don't forget to record each one and say "thank you" immediately.

Have you invited family friends to come in for tea and to see your gifts? It's a nice idea.

3 *days before:*

Send wedding information to society editors.

Relax, if possible.

Have going-away clothes pressed and ready.

Any out-of-town guests due today? See that they are met.

2 *days before:*

Check on final wedding details.

Review rehearsal procedure.

Is everything all set for the bridal dinner tomorrow
night? Place cards written? Your dress pressed?

1 day before:

Getting shivers of excitement? Take it easy! Have
your hair done. Get a manicure, and make it a
pale and demure shade of polish. See that
bridesmaids have the same.

How about writing a few thank-you notes?

Better review the wedding gifts so you'll know
their donors.

Pack all but last-minute things. Go to bridal dinner
and rehearsal. Have a marvelous time.

Your Wedding Day:

This is *it*. Have breakfast in bed, can't you? Stay
out of the way of caterers and their kitchen
crew. Check on the florist as he decorates for
the reception. Write some notes to keep your
mind off the Big Moment.

Be leisurely about your dressing but be ready in
plenty of time. Be moderate on the make-up.
Depend on that *someone* who is to zip you up,
to arrange your train and veil as you start down
the aisle.

It's fun, isn't it,

Best of luck!

Now that you have reviewed all the details of wedding
planning, let's go back to the beginning and set it all up
for your own special mapping out.

WHAT TYPE OF WEDDING FOR YOU?

This exciting decision really depends on your own
heart's desires, the size of your budget, the size of the
two families, and the number of relatives and guests
you'll want to include.

It's bound to be one of these:

1. The large formal wedding in a church, followed by home, hotel or country-club reception where everyone is invited.

2. The formal, semiformal or informal church or chapel wedding, followed by a small home or club reception to which only the families and intimate friends are invited.

3. The small wedding in a church, club or home to which only a few friends and the two families are asked, followed by a reception for everyone.

4. The garden, home or club wedding which includes reception for everyone.

5. The small chapel wedding without reception where bridal couple receive friends in foyer of the church or chapel.

6. The military wedding (usually formal) at the chapel on the army post or naval base, followed by a large reception at home or at the officers' club on the post.

But before you make the big decision, let's have a look at the financial obligations which belong to you and your family and those which belong to the bridegroom.

Responsibilities of the Bride's Family

1. The bride's personal and household trousseau.
2. The wedding ensemble (gown, veil, etc.).
3. The wedding invitations and enclosure cards.
4. Announcements.
5. The engagement and wedding photographs.
6. The bridesmaids' bouquets. (The bridegroom *may* pay for these if he wishes.)
7. The bridesmaids' gifts.
8. Gifts to musicians and other helpers who are friends.
9. The church expenses, except clergyman's fee, which include:
   aisle canvas (necessary for formal wedding)

and necessary for only
...ing)
...nd vocal)

10. I... family is not hosting the
a...

11. F... if you especially wish to
e... s (optional).

12. Housing of out-of-town bridal attendants and special guests.

13. Transportation of bridal party to and from church.

14. The wedding breakfast or reception (including music, food, catering, etc.).

15. Wedding gifts to the bride from all members of the immediate family.

The Bride's Personal Responsibilities

(This listing is for the bride who has a nest egg of her own and wishes to assume some of the financial obligations. Otherwise these responsibilities are included in the family budget.)

1. Groom's wedding ring, if it's a double-ring ceremony.
2. Small gifts for her attendants.
3. Wedding gift for the groom (optional).
4. Her medical examination.
5. Personal stationery and calling cards.
6. Her luggage.
7. Signing gift registry for wedding-present selections.

Responsibilities of the Bridegroom and His Family

1. Engagement and wedding rings.
2. His wedding clothes.
3. The marriage license.
4. The bride's bouquet and going-away corsage; bridesmaids' bouquets, boutonnieres for the men, and corsages for both mothers and grandmothers

(though the bride's family may correctly pay for all but the bride's flowers if they wish).

5. His medical examination.
6. Gifts for the bride, best man and ushers; groom may also provide accessories (ties and gloves) for the men attendants and both fathers in a strictly formal wedding (optional).
7. Luggage and necessaries for his personal wardrobe.
8. The bachelor dinner. (This is often given by the best man and ushers, or it may be a "Dutch-treat" party.) (optional)
9. Arrange billeting for groom's out-of-town attendants and their wives, and for guests of groom's family. (There is no obligation to pay hotel bills under normal circumstances.)
10. Bridal (or rehearsal) dinner, if given by bridegroom's parents (optional).
11. The clergyman's fee. (From $10 to $50 is customary, but the larger the wedding, the larger the fee.)
12. All honeymoon arrangements and expenses.

Note: Your joint responsibilities as a bridal couple include shopping for household necessities if you are setting up housekeeping soon after marriage. When you've decided where you are going to live and whether it's to be an apartment or a house, get a floor plan and work together on a mutually agreeable decorating scheme. Though the bride's family traditionally supplies the basics in a household trousseau, it is the groom who is responsible for providing the home itself, and equipping it with all the major furnishings. If you will be moving to another town, it is wise to consult movers and shippers somewhat in advance about the cost of packing, insuring and moving your wedding gifts and other household belongings, even though the move will probably not be made until after the wedding.

GET YOUR CALENDAR IN HAND

Now, let's consider the date for this important step of yours and decide on the time of day for the ceremony.

June, of course, is traditionally the bride's month, but statistics show that April, May and October also are coming into their own as chosen months for many fashionable weddings.

Marriage-license bureaus are busy every day of the year issuing the necessary documents, so it is purely a matter of your own personal taste and convenience.

Individual ministers are guided by their own preferences in the matter of dates, however, so consult your clergyman before you make your actual decision.

Saturday afternoons and evenings are the most popular of all days in the week because of convenience to business people. But if you want to choose Wednesday at four, or some other time that suits you, don't be influenced by what anyone else has done.

What Hour For the Wedding?

Most fashionable Catholic weddings, celebrated with a Nuptial High Mass, take place at noon. If you want Low Mass said, ten o'clock is a timely hour. If yours is an informal service to be held early in the morning, set the time for eight or nine. If it is to be the simplest of Catholic ceremonies celebrated in the church, without Mass, it may take place in the afternoon.

The most favored hours for Protestant ceremonies are at four or four-thirty in the afternoon and twelve or twelve-thirty for the morning wedding. Three-thirty is a nice hour if you are following the service with a simple teatime reception.

Easterners frown on the formal evening wedding, but it's very popular in the South because of the extreme daytime heat. The Middle West and Far West favor it largely because it offers an easy answer to the formal dress problem.

The invariable hours for the evening ceremony are eight, eight-thirty and nine o'clock.

You may make your own rules and set your time, unfettered by tradition, if you are having an informal affair. Your own convenience is the main thing to consider.

What Sort of Reception?

The high-noon wedding is apt to cost more than one in mid-afternoon, since the wedding breakfast which follows usually calls for a luncheon menu.

Weddings held late in the afternoon are generally followed by a reception supper, similar in bill of fare to the breakfast.

The reception following the three-thirty or four o'clock ceremony entails less expense if you limit refreshments to teatime food.

If you are budget-conscious, weigh all these pros and cons before you set the hour. This bit of forethought will help make your wedding add up to exactly what you want.

The degree of formality carried out in your wedding ceremony should be matched by the reception. A party of formal type should follow the formal church ceremony. A less formal function is in mood with the semiformal or informal ceremony.

Formality in entertaining does not mean fussiness or pomposity, however. It means carrying out correctness and charm and doing it with a flair.

SPECIAL TIPS TO MEMBERS OF BOTH FAMILIES

The Bride's Family

Family conferences on wedding issues are essential, with every member having a finger in the pie. Father, with his open checkbook, presides as the head of the house, and Mother with her check list is chairman of the arrangements committee, directing her corps of working aides in masterful fashion.

It's a time to delegate as many duties as possible to willing friends and relatives who wish to share in the excitement of wedding preparations. Bridesmaids may help in the addressing of invitations and announcements, if penmanship is passable. There's appointment-making, gift-listing, phone-answering, billeting and meeting of out-of-town guests that may wisely be turned over to trusted friends in order to leave the family free for other duties.

Mother's Responsibilities

As soon as wedding plans have been formed, the *bride's mother* should advise the bridegroom's mother of details, so that the latter may select her gown and make necessary plans.

She will work on the guest list with the bride and confer with the bridegroom's mother on his family's lists.

She will consult with the caterer (or maître d'hôtel if it's a club or hotel reception), get estimates from florists, engage the photographer, assist in shopping, help with the gift display—check and double check everything!

It is the mother's responsibility to see that there are cars to take the wedding party to and from church, to see that arrangements are made for housing out-of-town bridal attendants.

If the reception is not being held at the bride's home, it is the mother's duty, if she can so arrange it, to entertain with a tea or luncheon sometime before the wedding, so that friends may view the gifts.

If the bride's mother is a widow, she will act as both host and hostess, taking over a father's usual duties. She may, if she wishes, give her daughter in marriage by stepping forward from her pew, or merely rising in her place and answering "I do," when the minister asks, "Who giveth this woman to be married to this man?"

Dear Old Dad

The bride's father comes into his own as the official host at his daughter's wedding.

He necessarily must conform to the conventional dress decreed for the type of wedding chosen. If he doesn't own the correct attire, he should rent or borrow it. Otherwise the bride must change her plans and key her wedding to his wardrobe.

As head of the house, Father generally foots most of the bills for the wedding. For instance, there are floral decorations, bridesmaids' flowers, the musicians (the church sets the organist's fee, and it may run anywhere from $25 to $50), the sexton's fee or tip, which is in accordance with the elaborateness of the wedding ($5 to $10 is usually ample).

Is there to be a special traffic policeman? If so, Dad will want to fork over at least $10 or $15.

All the reception expenses are his responsibility—as are trousseau clothes if the bride has no nest egg of her own for such a purpose.

The bride and her father drive alone to the church, with a chauffeur or friend at the wheel. She is escorted up the aisle by him (on his right arm) and given in marriage at the altar.

He acts as host at the reception. He may or may not stand in the receiving line, but he remains throughout the reception until the last guests have been bidden good-by.

Don't forget that the right family attitude calls for pitching in joyfully on wedding plans, for such an attitude goes a long way toward making a calm, well-poised, *happy* bride at the altar!

The Groom's Family

"Look pleasant, please—and conform to the wedding plans set forth by the bride's family." That's the principal rule for the bridegroom's family to follow in wedding procedure.

As honor guests at their son's wedding the parents stand in the receiving line to meet all guests. They are dressed to conform with the rest of the wedding party.

In recent years, it has been customary for the bridegroom's family to give the bridal dinner or buffet supper on the evening of the rehearsal, thus relieving the bride's family of that extra activity during a very busy week. It is a gracious way for the new in-laws to entertain for the bridal pair and to become an integral part of the wedding.

The bridegroom's family pay their own traveling expenses and hotel bills if they live at a distance from the city in which the wedding is to take place. The bride's family may arrange the accommodations, but should not be expected to pay the bill.

As to their choice of a gift for the bride, the bridegroom's family should select something treasurable, if possible. Traditionally, it often is a silver tea service or a chest of flat silver in the chosen pattern. However, in this age of practical and casual living, it might more appropriately be a pair of electric blankets, or a living-room rug that would best suit the young couple.

At the bidding of the bride's mother, the groom's mother should comply promptly with her request for making up the invitation and announcement list. She is obliged to welcome the bride-to-be into the family as soon as she hears the good news.

If the families live in the same city, the groom's family should call upon the bride's family and welcome the bride to their home. If the bride lives in another city, a note of welcome is due her from the bridegroom's mother.

A reception or party of introduction is an appreciated gesture before the wedding (or following) if the bride is not known to friends of the groom's family. It is only courtesy that the bride's family be included by invitation to such an affair.

Reminders for the Groom

The lucky-in–love bridegroom should follow the lead of the bride in donning formal dress if it's to be a wedding of pomp and ceremony, and he should see to it that all the men in the wedding party (and both fathers) follow suit. Whatever the type of wedding, it is highly important that the men principals be correctly attired to conform with the mood set by the bride's gown.

The groom should hold early sessions with his little black memorandum book, his business, club and college directories in drawing up his wedding guest list. He should also prod his family into making out their lists giving full indications as to who is to be invited to the reception as well as the church, what special guests are to receive "Behind the ribbon" cards for up-front seating, with all details clearly defined.

Choose your best man and ushers with discretion and pride, then personally invite them in the early-planning stages, giving them a hint as to the type of wedding it is to be, so they will be prepared on the clothes situation. Gifts for the ushers are customarily small articles such as billfolds, cigarette cases, pens, cuff links or key rings, presented either at the bachelor dinner or the bridal dinner. The best man usually receives a bit more substantial gift than the others. As insurance that all the men will be uniformly dressed, the groom may provide them with identical ties, and gloves, also.

The wedding gift for the bride from her one-and-only should be something for her personal adornment, with a keep-sake quality, such as a string of pearls, a bracelet or pin—something she can cherish from her wedding day on.

The wedding ring should be chosen with the bride on hand. It should match the engagement ring in metal and in design, since the two rings are worn together on the same finger. The wedding ring is usually engraved on the inside with the initials of the groom first, *"J.B.W. to J.K.L.,"* with the wedding date following.

Half the fun of wedding planning is dreaming up the perfect honeymoon, with boy and girl poring over maps and setting dates well in advance. It's the groom's responsibility, of course, to make all reservations and pay all the bills for the trip.

A conference with the bride will be necessary to decide about the bridal bouquet and all the flowers for the wedding. It has been general wedding custom for the groom to pay for the bride's bouquet as well as for her going-away corsage, though she usually makes the selections. It has also long been the groom's responsibility to send corsages to the two mothers (and grandmothers, if any), after consulting with the bride as to their choices, and often to pay for the bridesmaids' bouquets, along with the boutonnieres for the best man, ushers, both fathers and himself.

In some communities, nowadays, there is a trend toward having the bride's family include all the wedding party bouquets and corsages in their order for the church and reception flowers, leaving only the bride's going-away corsage as the groom's responsibility. The gracious groom will conform to whatever plan seems best, after offering to accept his full responsibilities in flower ordering, according to tradition.

The all-important marriage license cannot be obtained without the preliminary tests, certificates, etc., and it is the obligation of the bridegroom to ferret out all legal information as to physical examinations, length of waiting period, birth certificates, baptismal certificates, etc., required in the locale where the couple plan to be married. The license itself should be obtained several weeks before the great day and kept in a special place until the time of the wedding, when it is entrusted to the care of the best man. As a special tip to the groom: Why not make a date with your bride-to-be ahead of time to treat her to a gay little champagne luncheon on the day you get your marriage license?

The *traditional* bachelor dinner is given by the groom for his best man and ushers, with other close friends attending. It is perfectly permissible, however, for the best man and ushers to give the party in the groom's honor, or it may be a "Dutch-treat" affair. Whatever the case, arrangements must be made for a time, place and menu, and invitations extended in plenty of time. The dinner should take place several days before the wedding so that it will not interfere with the rehearsal dinner or any family party.

To carry out sartorial perfection at the altar, the groom should make a note to have the soles of his new shoes blackened before he kneels beside the bride during the ceremony.

It's vital that the bridegroom take part in the wedding rehearsal, and it's his duty to notify his attendants of the time and the place for the rehearsal. A head usher should be selected by the groom, at the rehearsal, and he will want to see that all the men attendants are instructed as to their individual duties.

The groom should decide whether or not he is to kiss the bride at the altar—and let her in on the secret.

The clergyman's fee, entrusted to the best man on the day of the marriage, should be either in the form of crisp new bills or a check in a white envelope, presented to the clergyman by the best man either just before or after the ceremony.

The bride and groom both sign the wedding certificate, remember, and it should be cached away for safekeeping. Many couples have a photostatic copy made as a safeguard.

The thoughtful honeymooners remember to send thank-you telegrams to both sets of parents the next day after the wedding.

Do remember to do so!

CHAPTER 3 | Choosing Your Wedding Plan

Now that you know about everyone's responsibilities, let's make that big decision. It is *your* wedding, don't forget. It is not to be done for effect; nor to keep up with the Joneses. It is to express you, your own desires and inclinations, and to be in accordance with the type of life you are going to lead.

If your parents' scale of living is simple, don't make yourselves conspicuous by putting on a super de luxe affair that will pull at the family purse strings, and might subject you to criticism. Plan something simple and in good taste . . . in line with what you can comfortably afford.

IS IT TO BE A FORMAL CHURCH WEDDING?

If so, that doesn't mean it should be stiff or pompous. The word "formal" *is* rather misleading; "traditional" is more apt, as it applies to the procedure and dress regulations which are customarily accepted. For even formality has varying degrees.

If your social position, the size of your church and the state of your pocketbook warrant, your wedding may well be a large and elaborate affair with *all* the trimmings: confetti on the sidewalk, envelopes within envelopes, white gloves, and *you* as the star in a wedding gown with a long train.

It's a memory you'll cherish forever . . . the pictorial beauty of a perfect performance. The ultra-formal wedding!

Or again, it could be quite simple in its appointments, without flourish, and with only a small gathering of the clan at the church, yet carried out in formal tempo.

There are certain musts for any type of formal church wedding:

1. You must wear a formal wedding gown, preferably with a train, or floor-length.

2. The men in the wedding party must wear formal attire.

3. You must send engraved wedding invitations and reception cards. If it's a very large wedding, you will send such enclosures as "Behind the ribbons," and entrance cards to the church.

4. You must have an aisle canvas. You should have aisle ribbons and pew decorations.

5. You will need the services of a professional florist.

    5-A. You might want a professional photographer at the church door.

6. You must have a caterer to ease your mother's reception responsibilities.

7. You may or may not want a church canopy. It is desirable in case of rain, if the church entrance is not protected. Carpeted outside steps are customary.

8. Your family (or the bridegroom's) should entertain with a formal bridal dinner before the wedding. (Preferably the night before, with rehearsal following.)

9. You must have a maid of honor to attend you. You will probably want to have bridesmaids as well.

10. You must have ushers. (One for every twenty-

five to fifty guests is considered adequate in a large wedding.)

11. The bridegroom must have a best man.

12. You should be given in marriage by your father, if possible, or by an uncle or close family friend.

13. You should have a formal receiving line to greet guests at the reception.

14. You must have a bride's cake. You should have individual boxes for the wedding (or groom's) cake if it is quite formal.

15. You should have instrumental music at the reception.

16. You should have photographs taken of the bridal party. Candid shots during the reception are a happy solution.

17. You should toss your bridal bouquet during the reception as you leave to dress for going away.

18. Be sure to have real or fake rose petals ready for your guests to shower you two at going-away time . . . as you make a dash for your get-away car.

Any kind of important occasion takes some organizing, so don't let a few formal musts frighten you out of your original plans if a formal church wedding it is to be! The sooner you lay the foundations for your wedding structure, the faster and more firmly you'll be able to build toward its final conclusion.

Now let's see about further details.

If you plan to be married in your own church, in most cases there is no charge. If you have selected a church where you or your family are not members, there usually is a fee. Not all churches will allow non-parishioners to be married in them, so better check on church rules.

The bride usually chooses the church in which she wishes to be married, but it may just as well be the bridegroom's church.

You and your fiancé should call on the minister well in advance of the wedding. It's not only a courtesy but a canon-law requirement in the Roman Catholic, Greek Catholic and Protestant churches.

Besides your own minister chosen to officiate, you may also have an assisting clergyman in attendance at the altar if you wish. This is often done when a family friend or relative is a minister in another city, but it is necessary to arrange this in advance with the minister of the church where the wedding will be held.

The church organist generally has a set fee for church weddings. If you engage the choir or a church vocalist, handle the proceedings as you would any business proposition and engage all the musicians for the rehearsal as well as for the wedding, on terms confirmed in advance.

Perhaps you have some special friend whom you've always counted on to sing or play at your wedding. Talk this over with your minister to see if your plans conform with his particular standards. Plan to give the musician friend a gift if there is no regular fee for his services.

Check on the seating capacity of the church. Do not add more people to your invitation list than there is room to accommodate.

Take into consideration the amount of space that is available at the altar. Is there plenty of room for all your bridesmaids to show off to advantage? As we have said, a formal wedding presents opportunity for pretty pageantry. Make the most of this fact as you plan.

Visit your church and make a study of the physical effects. Note the color of walls, the shades used in the seat cushions, the predominating color tones in the stained-glass windows, the woodwork and the altar embellishments. If the background colors are extremely vivid and varied—or neutral and dull—be sure to jot down this information in your notebook. These details will be important when it comes time to choose your wedding colors.

Then observe the lighting facilities—daylight, electric light or candlelight. Does the church glow with flattering shadows as the afternoon sun wanes? Is the hour which you have tentatively set for the ceremony exactly right to take full advantage of this dramatic touch? Is the altar lighted by rich and beautiful transept windows that cast a soft warmth over the chancel at noontime?

Take all these things into consideration now while you are forming your plans and there is still time to make changes.

Look for a principal point of interest, a focal point, around which the church has been built.

If the architecture is modern, without the ornamentation of deeply colored glass windows, note this fact and plan the details of your wedding accordingly. It would be out of place to key your wedding to an old-fashioned theme in such a setting.

If your church is a small and simple structure, don't plan an elaborate processional, but keep your wedding simple.

Snow-white pillars, lavish gold decoration and blue-canopied ceilings, often found in the churches of early American design, inspire dreams of a Colonial wedding realistically come true.

Make a point of looking up the sexton while you are taking notes at the church. You can confer with him on important details such as fire laws, bell ringing, the aisle canvas, stair carpet and such. He will know the church's rules on permitting candlelight weddings, if that happens to be part of your plan. Take down his name and telephone number. You may need him later.

Is a prayer bench used in this particular church? If it is supplied by the church, you will be saved an item of expense at the florist's. See if candelabra are available for wedding services. The sexton will know. Your florist will supply them, and also the tapers, if the church does not have them.

Notify the florist and the church secretary as to the number of pews to be marked off for special guests.

Arrival at the Church

The ushers should arrive one hour before the ceremony and take their places at each inner door leading from the vestibule, as directed by the head usher. Guest lists should be distributed by the head usher to selected ushers. If flowers are delivered to the church, the sexton should see that all members of the wedding party receive their boutonnieres.

The bridegroom and the best man should arrive together at the church a half hour before the ceremony, receive their boutonnieres and go directly to the vestry. The best man takes the bridegroom's hat and coat (and his own) to the vestibule preceding the ceremony and leaves them in care of the sexton.

The bridesmaids and other bridal attendants should arrive together at least ten minutes before the appointed time of the ceremony and retire to rooms which adjoin the vestibule to await the bride and her father, who will follow immediately in the next car. In cases where the bride and her attendants dress at the church, they should all assemble in the vestibule of the church three or four minutes before the signal for the wedding march is given. The bride's father joins the wedding party there.

The bridegroom's family usually arrives at the church about eight or ten minutes before time for the ceremony.

Is there a suitable place at the church for you and your attendants to dress for the wedding?

Lucky *you* if there is. Your wedding ensemble and bridesmaids' costumes can be sent on hangers directly to the church from the store. They should be delivered early on the day of your wedding and cared for by the sexton in the dressing-rooms provided for this purpose. Someone should check their delivery and spread a clean white sheet on the dressing-room floor. Then everything will be in readiness for you and the bridesmaids to saunter in at least two hours before the ceremony and dress in perfect leisure—with never a fear of a wrinkle as you walk down the aisle. You can arrange to have on hand your hairdresser, and the bridal counselor (or whoever is to help you dress).

The bride's mother goes to the church with other members of her family; she is escorted to her place of honor one minute before the wedding march begins.

Preliminaries to the Ceremony

The introductory music begins about a half hour before the ceremony. Vocal solos or choral services should be scheduled to take place during the last few minutes before ceremony time, after most of the guests have arrived and are seated.

Candles should be lighted by the sexton before guests arrive, unless a traditional candle-lighting service is to be performed.

Reserved pews for special guests usually number from ten to twenty, depending on the size of the church, and pew cards are presented by guests to the ushers at the door.

About five minutes before time for the ceremony, the bridegroom's mother is escorted to her place in the first pew on the right side. The bridegroom's father follows a pace behind and takes his place in the pew beside her. Both leave outer wraps with the sexton in the vestibule, but the mothers wear their hats (or appropriate head coverings) and gloves throughout the ceremony.

The bride's mother is escorted to her place in the first pew on the left about one minute before the ceremony begins. No one is seated by an usher after she takes her place.

When guests arrive after the ceremony starts, they should go directly to the gallery and seat themselves or remain in the rear of the church.

If aisle ribbons are used, two ushers walk to the front of the church, where ribbons are attached on the front pews, and draw them over the tops of the pews, all the way to the back of the church.

If the aisle canvas has not already been tacked down by the florist, it should be attended to by the ushers. As soon as the pair of ushers drawing the ribbons has returned to the back of the church, another pair of ushers should go to the front of the church and draw the canvas along the aisle. It will have been folded, accordion fashion, so that it unfolds easily as the ushers walk back along the aisle, holding the outside corner of the canvas strip and drawing it behind them as they go.

The wedding march signal should be given to the organist by the sexton when the procession is ready to start.

If the congregation stands during a wedding ceremony in your church, all guests follow the lead of the bride's and groom's families and rise at the first note of the wedding march. They remain standing until the minister indicates that everyone be seated.

Procedure for Leaving the Church

The bride's car (the same one in which she arrived with her father at the church) should await her and the bridegroom at the curb. It is the first car to leave the church.

Next come the cars filled with bridesmaids and the best man; third, the parents of the bride; and fourth, the parents of the groom, followed by the cars occupied by immediate families of both the bride and the groom, the clergyman, ushers and other guests.

THE FORMAL HOME WEDDING

If it is to be a home wedding, the plan can be flavored with much intimate charm and sentiment . . . yet still be keyed to the formal symbols.

There's the wide winding stairway, railed with the banister where you used to go tumbling and sliding. There's the big spacious living room (your vows will be spoken there) . . . filled with all your endearing memories of gay family gatherings. There's something sort of nostalgic about it all—and terribly, terribly thrilling.

Now step back and take a look around. (We must be practical, you know.)

Is there plenty of space for everyone you want to invite?

Can the French doors be opened and the screened porch used?

Will you wear ice-blue to match the blue of the ceiling?

Ideas will come burgeoning right and left once you begin.

Look back on pages 38-45, at the list of "musts" for the formal church wedding. The same measuring stick is used, the same rules apply, except that you can *eliminate:*

> A canopy (unless it's extreme weather and you want to be luxurious).
>
> Separate cards, "Behind the ribbons" and entrance cards.
>
> A professional florist if your garden is overflowing with flowers and someone in the family has a special knack for decorating.

You'll send the same sort of formal invitations, wear a wedding gown and a train, and decide for yourself whether ushers are necessary.

A special point to consider is your caterer. You will need somebody *capable* to lift this responsibility off your mother's shoulders. If you can afford professional help, you'll find it well worth the money.

Keep a Home Atmosphere

The charm of a house wedding is that it is *your* home and reflects your own special atmosphere.

Unless it is necessary to accommodate all the guests, don't move out all the furniture and give the appearance of a rented ballroom. Leave the sofas, a few occasional chairs and tables (they can be moved back against the wall), and don't do away with all the lamps. Remove the small objects and any of the pictures which interfere with your decorative effects.

If she wishes, your mother may stand near the door to receive wedding guests as they arrive. Or if she prefers to remain with you and your attendants until just before the ceremony, she may delegate a close friend or relative to this duty, and later personally greet everyone in the receiving line. She should take her place in the front row, to the left of the altar, just before time for the ceremony to start. In a home wedding your mother, as the hostess, usually does not wear hat or gloves. Members of the bridegroom's family are shown to their places in the front row, at right of the altar, when they arrive for the wedding.

When the clergyman arrives, he should be escorted to a room which has been reserved for him, the groom and the best man.

Your fireplace in the living room or a large window will provide a suitable background for the ceremony. But make certain that you select the setting which serves as a central point for everyone. No wedding guest wants to be crowded out of seeing the ceremonial proceedings.

It is not unusual in a home wedding to omit an altar arrangement and have, instead, a *prie-dieu* against a background of greenery and flowers. Kneeling benches may be borrowed from a church, a florist or a church supply house. An altar may be easily improvised, however, by covering a small table with a square of fine white silk, linen or lace. Or you may wish to borrow a real altar frontal from your church.

If you can arrange it, the altar should be so situated that the bridegroom and his attendant may come from a door on the right. This eliminates the awkwardness of crossing in front of the altar as they take their places on the right side.

If you want a background of organ music for your formal wedding at home—and nothing is more appropriate—don't despair. The rental department of almost every large music store is equipped with desk-sized electric organs, and the rental charge isn't at all prohibitive. You can get a professional organist (perhaps from the same music company) for a reasonable fee.

If not organ music, you might have a harpist or a string trio with piano accompaniment.

A small choir of young boys, or of feminine voices, chanting the wedding march to organ or piano accom-

paniment, offers a beautiful and impressive variation to
the usual instrumental solo.

Processional and Recessional

The wedding procession for a formal home wedding
follows in the same order as the church wedding procession.

At the close of the ceremony, the groom usually
kisses the bride, the minister congratulates the bridegroom and gives felicitations to the bride, then with-
draws. The couple then turns to receive greetings from
both sets of parents, after which a receiving group is
formed in front of the altar.

THE CLUB OR HOTEL WEDDING

A club or hotel wedding is treated in much the same
manner as a home wedding. It may lack the personal
background, but it can be very dignified and lovely in its
appointments.

It means that you put many of your contingent problems into the hands of experts—which is often a welcome plan. Clubs and hotels usually do not charge for
the rooms used if they are commissioned to do the catering.

Meet with the maître d'hôtel and engage the ballroom
or other rooms suitable for the ceremony and reception.
Consult your florist and go with him to the scene of the
wedding to discuss decorations.

Get estimates on everything and confirm your orders
in writing.

See about your music, approve the reception menu
and go about making your plans just as outlined for a
formal home wedding.

Your mother may receive the guests as they arrive,
then take her proper place on the left side of the improvised altar. Other members of the family who are not in
the bridal party mingle with the guests before the cere-

mony, as do the parents and immediate family of the groom.

The place you select for the ceremony depends on the shape of the room and the convenience of the occasion. If no aisleway is marked off, the ushers should see to it that an aisle space is indicated just before ceremony time. Or the aisleway could be formed by having four or six of your friends (two or three on each side) carry ropes of greenery and flowers which could be stretched to form a pathway to the altar.

If you prefer to have only a short distance to walk to the altar, you may enter from a doorway at the left of the altar, preceded by your attendants, if there are to be any.

In a simpler ceremony you may choose to greet your own guests and step up to the altar naturally and easily, with the bridegroom at your side.

WHAT TO WEAR FOR A FORMAL DAYTIME WEDDING

Bride: Wedding gown with cathedral or shorter length train; long or short veil. Long gloves for short sleeves, otherwise optional. Dress fabric suitable to season, with satin still the traditional favorite. White, antique or pastel shade. Shoes to match gown. Pale hose. Bridal bouquet or white prayer book. Real jewelry in good taste.

Bridal Attendants: Long or short dresses, with shoulder covering, generally in the same style. Colors may be matching or harmonizing. Gloves customary if sleeves are short. Bouquets to match, usually, though maid of honor or matron of honor's flowers may be individually designed.

Bridegroom: Cutaway coat, striped trousers, silk top hat. Formal gray or beige waistcoat (white piqué in summer). Pleated shirt with starched collar (turned-down or wing), Ascot or four-in-hand tie.

Black patent or calf shoes, black hose (spats optional). Doeskin gloves to match waistcoat. Boutonniere is usually a sprig from the bride's bouquet, such as: lilies of the valley, stephanotis or white violets.

Best Man, Ushers, Fathers: The same as groom, with individual variations such as width of trouser stripes, turned-down collar (groom and best man usually are the only ones who wear wing collars in the wedding party). Neckwear and gloves of ushers should be uniform. Boutonnieres differ. Best man and bride's father may wear gardenias.

Mothers: Both dresses should be the same length in flattering colors that go well with the bridal party. White or off-white kid gloves. Corsages.

Women Guests: Street-length dresses or long ones. White kid gloves.

In many churches, hats or head coverings are not mandatory.

Men Guests: Men may wear formal afternoon clothes like the ushers, or Oxford jackets, though dark blue or gray business suits are more casual.

WHAT TO WEAR FOR A FORMAL EVENING WEDDING

Bride: Same costume as formal daytime wedding. Conservative décolletage. With short sleeves, wear opera-length white kid gloves. Long veil (a yard longer than train) is more formal than short veil. Bridal bouquet or white prayer book. Diamond or pearl jewelry.

Attendants: Long or short dresses as decreed by the bride. All must be the same length.

Groom: Full evening dress: white tie and tails after
6:00 P.M. the year around. Black or midnight
blue. High silk or opera hat. White waistcoat,
white bow tie, stiff shirt, wing collar, white kid
gloves. White or black pearl studs. Patent-leather
pumps or Oxfords, black hose. Boutonniere, same
as formal daytime.

Best Man, Ushers, Fathers: Full evening dress, the
same as groom. Boutonnieres same as formal daytime wedding.

Mothers and Women Guests: Formal evening gowns,
long or short, with opera-length white kid gloves.
Real jewelry. Mothers: Corsages to harmonize
with dresses.

Men Guests: Full evening dress preferred; black tie
and dinner jacket permissible.

THE SEMIFORMAL WEDDING

Your wedding, in semiformal tempo, may be as exquisite and intimate as you want to make it.

It should strike a happy medium, in dress and procedure, between the highly formal and the very casual
types. It offers you more opportunity for variation than
the formal wedding.

Your list of "musts" is cut down considerably. As a
realist, you will forego the opulence of a trumpet-
flourishing wedding, but you will walk up a church aisle
in the legendary beauty of bridal tradition.

You may choose a short or full-length wedding gown
that can be worn on other occasions. You may wear a
veil and all the other traditional bridal accessories, and
carry a wedding bouquet, a dainty sheath of blossoms
or a prayer book on which is an orchid or floral spray—
whatever is in keeping with the simplicity of your gown.

Most young men rent striped trousers and Oxford

gray jackets or dinner jackets, if it's an evening affair. For summertime, they may don white jackets with dark trousers, or white suits for daytime affairs; white dinner jackets after 6:00 P.M.

Of course you may have attendants (try to limit them to three or four at the most) in festive gowns, but not too formal.

You may skip the aisle canvas if you are not wearing a train, and don't even consider a canopy if semiformality and simplicity are the theme.

The semiformal wedding may be held in a church or chapel, at your home or club. It may even be a garden wedding.

Make your floral decorations beautiful in their simplicity. Call in a florist, if you must, but use discernment in whatever you plan.

If you are thirtyish, or if this is a second venture into matrimony, why not wear a lovely gown of pastel or jewel tones, and have richly shaded flowers in your corsage or bouquet.

Send engraved invitations (the small, less formal kind) if your guest list totals more than fifty, or send them even for a smaller wedding if expense isn't an item. If only a very few close friends and relatives are to come, then phone them orally or send handwritten notes which your mother may write. If you wish to send some of the invitations under your own name, that's also permissible, but your mother and father are your sponsors, remember, so mention them in a gracious way somewhere in your note.

Issue the invitations (either kind) about three weeks before the wedding.

WHAT TO WEAR FOR A SEMIFORMAL DAYTIME WEDDING

Bride: Short-trained floor-length or waltz-length gown of white or pastel shade. Fingertip veil or veil-less headdress. Shoes to match gown. Bridal bouquet or white prayer book. Conservative jewelry.

Attendants: Long or short dresses, customarily matching in style. Colors matching or harmonizing. Long or short gloves optional. Matching or contrasting accessories. Bouquets becoming to dresses. Maid or matron of honor: may match or contrast in style and color with the bridesmaids.

Bridegroom: Oxford jacket, striped trousers, matching vest or light gray double-breasted vest, white shirt, four-in-hand or bow tie, gloves optional. Lily of the valley boutonniere. Summer: all white suit or light flannels with dark jacket; or light jacket with dark trousers. It is never correct for men to wear a summer tuxedo in daytime wedding before 6:00 P.M.

Best Man, Ushers, Fathers: All men of wedding party follow lead of the groom. Boutonnieres same as formal wedding for the men.

Mothers: Full length or short cocktail-type dresses, worn with gloves, hats or headdresses of some sort, and corsages.

Women Guests: Street-length dresses or ensembles are appropriate.

Men Guests: Oxford jackets and striped trousers or dark business suits. Summer: tropical suits, light flannels and dark coats, or white jackets with dark trousers.

WHAT TO WEAR FOR A SEMIFORMAL EVENING WEDDING

Bride: Short-trained or trainless wedding gown of white or pastel shade. Fingertip veil or headdress. Shoes to match. Bridal bouquet or white prayer book. Jewelry in good taste.

Attendants: Long or short dresses, matching or contrasting in color; all the same style for bridesmaids. Long or short white kid gloves. Matching accessories. Bouquets. Maid or matron of honor: long or short gown to match bridesmaids in style. Color may complement. Bouquet to conform with others.

Bridegroom: Dinner jacket and black tie is accepted for semiformal evening wear in most communities. Accessories: cummerbund, bow tie, white pleated or plain shirt. Black patent oxfords, black hose. Lily-of-the-valley or gardenia boutonniere. Summer: white dinner jacket, black trousers; all white suit or light flannels with dark jackets.

Best Man, Ushers, Fathers: All men of the wedding party follow lead of the groom. Best man wears gardenia and ushers wear white carnations as boutonnieres.

Mothers: Conservative evening gowns in long or short styles, long gloves and corsages.

Women Guests: Long or short dresses, semiformal styles if invited to reception following the ceremony. Street-length costumes if going only to the church.

Men Guests: Dinner jackets usual for all seasons (white in summer) if going to reception. Also acceptable: dark business suits or lighter suits for summer.

THE INFORMAL WEDDING

You may be one of those couples who prefer to be married strictly without fuss. You want to wear your going-away costume or an afternoon dress and have another couple "stand up" with you at the altar. Yet you want the simplest of ceremonies in the presence of a mere handful of people.

Perhaps it's a spur-of-the-moment occasion with no time to get ready for a big wedding.

You can still make it memorable and impressive in chapel, at home, in your garden or at your club.

Decide on all the fundamentals and—if possible—at least two weeks before the date you and your mother should call the guests and write notes to out-of-town relatives and friends.

Hold yourself down to one attendant each (a maid of honor for you and a best man for the groom). Walk to the altar beside your maid of honor for moral support if you choose.

Have some sort of music if you can possibly arrange it. All the masterpieces in wedding music are available on phonograph records. Have you thought of that?

Keep the decorations simple, with greenery and a few flowers at the altar to blend with the color scheme of your clothes. Autumn leaves could be used in containers at the altar if it's a fall marriage. Evergreens and holly are festive for the Christmas season, informal garden flowers in soft colors for summer.

If it's a church wedding, dispense with aisle decorations or pew markings. Don't march down a long aisle if only a few seats in the church are to be occupied. Enter from the side door at the left of the altar with your maid of honor or following her. The bridegroom and the best man will come from the vestry door on the right in the usual manner.

Stop at the back of the church and greet your guests before dashing away if there is to be no get-together afterward.

If there's to be a breakfast or a small reception, don't plan anything sumptuous, but make it very informal and gay. It might be a buffet or a simple tea at your family's home with your wedding cake as the main attraction. Or you could engage a small private dining room in a hotel or restaurant for the gathering.

This is the easiest sort of wedding to have if you

don't mind foregoing some of the traditional touches. It may still have true dignity and beauty, which are always essential to any sort of wedding.

Here are a few ideas to start you thinking along your own lines:

1. Wear a creamy-white sheer wool dress with matching hat if it's wintertime and you want to live up to some of the bridal traditions. Exchange vows before a lovely hearth fire.

2. If you are wearing your traveling costume in a fall or winter church wedding, carry a tiny fur muff adorned with a single orchid.

3. Have a late afternoon ceremony in the shadow of the Christmas tree lights during the holiday season. Add a touch of mistletoe or holly to your shoulder corsage as a festive touch.

4. If it's springtime or summer, top your outfit with a light-hearted hat made entirely of white flowers draped with a wispy white veil and have your corsage made of the real flowers to match. You might choose a shaded porch or the cool shelter of a great spreading tree as the scene of the ceremony.

WHAT TO WEAR FOR AN INFORMAL DAYTIME OR EVENING WEDDING

Bride: Street-length dress or going-away outfit, worn with hat . . . or hatless. Gloves optional. Harmonizing accessories. Corsage, or carry small bouquet. Conservative jewelry.

Attendants: Usually one or two attendants only. Dresses same length as bride's. Corsages or small bouquets. Suitable accessories.

Bridegroom: Dark-gray or blue business suit, white shirt, black shoes, conservative tie and socks. Boutonniere: maroon carnation. Summer: dark tropical suit, or light trousers with dark jacket, or natural-colored jacket with dark trousers.

Best Man, Ushers, Fathers: All wear business suits, following lead of the bridegroom. Carnation boutonnieres.

Mothers and Women Guests: Afternoon dresses, street-length. Mothers may wear corsages.

Men Guests: All wear business suits for informal weddings.

THE MILITARY WEDDING

You will parade under the shining blades of your serviceman's ushers, who will be in uniform. That, in brief, is the outstanding difference between the civilian and military ceremonics.

You will follow the same suggested pattern of the formal church wedding, if that is the type you have chosen. The basic structure of the wedding is the same as that of any other wedding. It is classified as "military" when the groom is a member of the armed services and chooses ushers from among his military friends only. The best man may or may not be a civilian. If he is a civilian, he and the bride's father (or whoever gives her in marriage) should wear formal attire.

If the bridegroom is a West Point graduate, a Naval Academy man or Air Force officer, he presents his bride with a miniature of his own class ring, set either with a smaller stone similar to his or a diamond. This, according to military custom, is her engagement ring.

If you are an Army or Navy daughter, steeped in the customs of the service, you doubtless will want to have all the fanfare of a true military wedding.

If you live with your parents on a post, you probably will wish to have the chaplain officiate at the wedding. All garrison officers and their wives are usually invited to both the ceremony and the reception.

If you are not an Army daughter and the wedding is not held on the post, you should see to it that the groom's post commander and his commanding officer are invited with their wives.

Likewise, in a Navy or Air Force wedding which is not held on a base, it is customary to invite the groom's commanding officer, his executive officer and the head of his department.

Decorations: Usually the bride and groom stand under the national and regimental colors or unit standard, arranged with the decorations at the altar. These flags may be crossed or stand separately. White flowers may be used at the altar, as well as aisle-post decorations for formal weddings.

The wedding procession differs very little from any civilian ceremony procession, but the recessional is distinctive. At the close of the wedding ceremony, the ushers, remaining in their same positions, draw their swords at the command, "Draw sabers" (from one of the ushers). The bride and groom pass under the arch, followed by the maid of honor and the best man and then the bridesmaids by twos. They proceed up the aisle while the ushers go out the side door, hasten to the chapel steps and again form the arch of swords for the bridal party to pass under as they leave the chapel.

If you prefer, it is equally correct to have the ushers escort the bridesmaids in the recessional, after the bride and groom have passed under the arch. As is customary, the bridegroom, best man and groomsmen each offer their right arms to bride, maid of honor and bridesmaids respectively, thus avoiding any entanglement of sabers and dresses and leaving their left hand free to carry their caps, which are held with the visor pointing left oblique.

Military Protocol Reminders

The bride and groom together cut the bride's cake with saber or sword. After the wedding party is seated at the bridal table, if it's a sit-down affair, other guests are seated according to military rank.

The arch of swords or sabers is for commissioned officers only.

There is no rule prompting anyone to have a strictly military wedding merely because the bridegroom happens to be in the service.

Reserve officers do not have military weddings unless they are on active duty.

Military Dress Regulations

In a very formal wedding during peacetime, Army, Air Force and Navy personnel may wear dress uniforms. During a period of war and national emergency, however, officers after graduation are not required to include formal dress uniforms, so may wear regulation uniforms at their weddings. All military members wear side arms and leave their caps in the vestibule. No boutonnieres are worn with uniforms.

The entire wedding party should conform to formal or informal dress, according to the mood set by the uniforms. Civilian guests wear formal daytime or evening dress at formal military weddings, business suits for informal weddings.

Medal ribbons may be worn with the regulation uniforms. Large medals are worn with dress uniforms. Miniature medals are worn with non-dress uniforms, on the left lapel.

THE GARDEN WEDDING

An exchange of vows under clear blue skies. How perfect!

The only drawback is that the skies cannot always be counted on to be clear blue, and no one ever heard of a bride carrying an umbrella down the aisle.

The only thing to do is to plan two altars instead of one. One for the garden and the other for indoors in case of rain. Since your house will be in order anyway, it will require very little trouble to move the kneeling bench and altar arrangement of flowers inside if the weather is threatening. The important point is to be prepared.

A garden wedding may be strictly formal, semiformal or informal. It all depends on the type of clothes you wear.

If you choose a wedding gown with long train, with the men in formal attire, follow the rules set down for the formal home wedding.

If the bridegroom and his attendants want to wear light summer suits, wear a simpler wedding gown, either short, or floor length, and make it semiformal in mood.

If you want to wear a street-length dress of white or light pastel of the informal sort, the men may wear light summer clothes. There is much latitude offered in such a wedding.

An aisle canvas should outline the way to the altar for the formal wedding. You may have it for the semi-formal wedding if you wish.

In these days of vitamin treatment for flowers, a host of plants may be transplanted while they are in bloom to glorify your garden if you need them. And trellises may be arranged and planted with trailing vines.

For the less elaborate affair, the smooth green lawn will serve as a setting for the sort of wedding everyone enjoys.

A clump of bushes, a niche in a garden wall, a columned summerhouse or the shade of a lovely big tree will serve as a beautiful background for the ceremony.

Look about the garden and decide on a spot for the altar. Try to arrange it so that guests may view the ceremony without facing the sun if possible.

Add the charm of color—pedestals of flowers or garlands of green outlining the aisle pathway . . . your bridal party in frothy frocks as debonair as a summer breeze.

Place the punch bowl and table under the rose arbor, or arrange to have buffet service in the summerhouse. Serve your wedding repast at small tables under a marquee in another part of the garden, if the occasion is to be that elaborate. Or have guests proceed to the porch or a shaded terrace for light refreshments.

THE DOUBLE WEDDING

A double wedding ceremony with its sweet sentiment and beautiful pageantry offers twice as much opportunity for developing your ideas as a single wedding.

It may be carried out in formal, semiformal or informal mood—however you wish it. The brides may be sisters or very close friends. Each usually has her own wedding party group to precede her to the altar.

Harmony of color and style in the matter of clothes is important, but the brides do not have to be dressed exactly alike, nor do their respective attendants.

If the brides are sisters, the older one is given in marriage by her father and precedes the younger sister to the altar. The second bride may be escorted by her brother, uncle or near relative.

If there is an unusually wide aisle, both sisters may be escorted by their father, one on each arm.

If the brides are friends, instead of sisters, each father gives his own daughter in marriage.

Be sure to select a church with ample altar space (if it's to be a church wedding) before you arrange for a large number of attendants. In one double wedding of note, the brides, who were sisters, served as maid and matron of honor to each other. This arrangement lessened the size of the wedding party, yet furnished the required number of witnesses and was doubly impressive.

IF IT IS ALTAR TRIP NUMBER TWO

If this is your second entrance into marriage, let it be a memorable occasion. Naturally you will not plan a big wedding, so why not make it an event of sweet simplicity, dignity and tradition, "to be remembered as long as you both shall live"?

You might like to wear a daytime dress in a lovely

pastel or in a deep, rich color. Or perhaps you prefer to be married in your going-away outfit, with a corsage of course. You can be a very pretty bride and still not wear white, you know.

Even though you may have been married very young and soon widowed, even though you may feel that you were cheated out of having a big fancy wedding—don't consider white for a second wedding. A bridal veil is never worn if you have been married before.

In every other respect, however, you may follow many of the tenets and traditions of a semiformal or informal wedding. Your family may send out engraved invitations, just as in a first marriage. More often guests are invited orally or by informal notes. Or you may have your parents send out announcements only.

Your father may give you away, even though he may have done so in your first wedding. You may be married in a church, chapel or at home or club. Your decorations follow the same style suggested for any informal wedding, as does the time of your wedding.

Your groom will have a best man, and may have ushers if occasion demands. You may have a maid or matron of honor, but don't have a great number of bridesmaids. You don't have to have *any*. If you are a widow, you may wish to have your own daughter as flower girl or maid of honor with you in the wedding.

If it is the groom's second marriage and the bride's first, the wedding plans may be of a more formal nature and still remain in good taste. It is unlikely, however, that a bride will want to celebrate with too much fanfare. Good common sense, local custom and the dictates of your church will all come in good stead.

THE OLDER BRIDE

If the older bride who has always dreamed of being married in white is youthful enough in appearance, she may avoid criticism by deciding on a semiformal wedding rather than a large formal ceremony.

She could select a white gown of traditional style with

no train, or a short one, and carry out all conforming details. White flowers simply arranged in her hair would be charming.

A large reception is in perfect order following a church ceremony. The bride may be given in marriage by her father and be attended by both maid of honor and bridesmaids. Junior bridesmaids or flower girls make lovely attendants for the older bride, but the number in the wedding party should be held down reasonably in any case.

THE CIVIL CEREMONY

If, for your own special reasons, you and your bridegroom wish to evade all wedding fanfare, you may go quietly to a county clerk or a judge or the justice of the peace to exchange your vows.

A street-length dress or an ensemble is customary for a ceremony at the courthouse or at the home or office of the Justice of the Peace. When you are married at the home of a judge however, you may wear a long dress and be attended by a maid or matron of honor if you wish.

In any circumstances you may have a reception or wedding breakfast for any number of friends following this kind of quiet ceremony.

SPECIAL QUESTIONS AND ANSWERS

What Type of Wedding Is Appropriate

. . . when one of the families is in mourning?
If there has been a death in either the bride's or the bridegroom's immediate family within a period of less than ten months, a large ultraformal wedding should not be considered. If the bride is so disposed, however, there is no reason why she cannot have a smallish wedding in the formal mood either in church or at home six months after a death has occurred.

... when a girl in moderate circumstances
marries a wealthy man?

The bride's family should plan a wedding that is in complete accord with the family's circumstances, and financial aid should never be accepted from the groom or his family. The groom's mother may give a large reception for the bridal pair if she wishes, but not on the wedding day.

... when the bridal couple wishes to hold
the ceremony in their new home?

If there is no alternative but a county clerk's unromantic office, by all means don't hesitate. This is an irregularity in the world of wedding etiquette, but one that is understandable to your friends. However, make certain in such circumstances that your mother or a close relative is present to sponsor the occasion and act as hostess at the wedding and the reception.

... when the bride's parents are divorced?

Here's where the most gracious way of coping with a situation is the correct way, and where sensitive feelings must be carefully considered.

It is perfectly permissible for a bride to be given in marriage by her divorced father if she so desires, even though her mother, with whom she lives, has married again. The invitations should be issued by the mother only. But the reception cards will be in the name of the mother and her second husband, since he will act as host for the reception.

The bride's father is unlikely to go to the reception, but again he may, accompanied by his second wife, if there is a friendly feeling between the two families.

After the bride's father (in these circumstances) has given her in marriage at the altar, he retires by a side aisle into a rear pew.

On the other hand, if the bride is not close to her own father, she may be given in marriage by her stepfather, an uncle or whomever she chooses.

Invitations or announcements may be sent in both the mother and stepfather's name if the stepfather is to sponsor the bride through her entire wedding. The invitations may even read "request the honour of your presence at the marriage of *their* daughter" if the bride's own father is out of the picture.

If the bride-to-be lives with her father, he should sponsor her marriage. Whether or not her mother attends the wedding is a matter to be settled individually.

CHAPTER 4 | The Honour of Your Presence Is Requested

Invitations are as much a part of wedding tradition as the bridal veil itself. Even though yours is to be an informal occasion, if other than close friends and relatives are going to be there, you will want to send out the formal kind. It's logical that you (or your mother) wouldn't wish to telephone or send informal notes to a large group of casual friends or mere acquaintances—as you would do in the case of a very small wedding.

Traditional forms are rigid as invitations go, so there is little chance of going astray in their selection. Today we find that there are many other forms of wording that are acceptable but the general composition or needed information remains the same. The size and type of lettering may vary and you will have a large selection to choose from.

Announcements and invitations should always be raised lettering to be correct, and the quality of paper should be of the best.

MAKING UP YOUR LISTS

Both families (yours and the bridegroom's) contribute to the invitation list, and the time to start working on them is at once.

It is one thing, above all, that shouldn't be done haphazardly.

Consult your old address books. Start on a neighborhood list, your school list, a club list, a relative list, Christmas-card lists and a friend list. Then get the same tabulation from the groom's family.

If your wedding is in church and your reception at home, it is wise to make two separate lists—one for those who are to receive invitations to the wedding only, another for those who are to be included in the reception.

When you do your final pruning, try not to cut down too rigidly. Everyone loves to see a wedding and to dance at one. It's gracious custom in a large formal wedding to include old friends of the family who knew you when you were a child, servants of long standing, your seamstress and all those to whom your wedding has special sentimental significance.

Guests invited only to the church are under no obligations to send gifts, you know, if there is to be a reception. But an invitation to the wedding reception automatically calls for a present.

Don't include on your list people whom you or your family do not really know, and never try to pay off social obligations with invitations to your reception.

WHO ISSUES THE INVITATIONS?

Your parents should issue the invitations and announcements, even though you are not living at home. If your parents are not living, your aunt and uncle or nearest relatives may sponsor your wedding. A close friend or guardian may issue them if it seems feasible. An older bride and groom often send their own announcements.

FORM OF INVITATION

There is a variety in paper sizes and colorings, with enclosure cards to correspond. Traditionally the paper used has been snow-white opaque paper, ivory or parchments, but today you will find many new colors and types of paper available. The large folded square is usually associated with the formal wedding and the smaller size, with the less formal one.

There are many popular lettering styles available and any reliable source of invitations knows what is correct and will have a wide selection for you to see.

Two envelopes are used, the inside one to enclose the invitation or announcement and the accompanying cards; the outside one for addressing and to protect the enclosures. Order your thank you notepaper while you are ordering your invitations. You may use informals (those folded cards with your names imprinted on the outside), or small folded sheets of stationery or anything that is currently in vogue. Check your invitation lists for the number you will need. Have your stationery monogrammed if you wish with your maiden initials for notes to be sent before the wedding. Obviously your married monogram should never be used until after your name has been changed.

If your wedding is to be small and you plan to send handwritten notes, select good quality white linen stationery in small folded sheets.

Wording of Invitation

1. "Request the honour of your presence" is generally the accepted form to use for church wedding invitations. The word "honour," you'll notice, is spelled with a *u*.

2. "Request the pleasure of your company" is used for a home, club or hotel wedding, since invitations include the reception following the ceremony.

3. First names should be written in full, as initials do not identify sufficiently. Nicknames are never used.

4. Don't abbreviate titles other than *Mr., Mrs.,* and *Dr. Junior* should be spelled in full if space permits.

5. When invitations or announcements are issued by anyone other than the parents of the bride, her full name should be used.

6. The name of the bride should be prefixed by *Miss* if the invitations are issued by someone who is not related to the bride. If it is a second marriage for a young woman, her parents may send the invitations or announcements without the prefix *Mrs.*—but will use her married name.

7. Your street address may be engraved under the name of the church, but it usually is not necessary.

8. "Daylight-saving time" may be engraved after the time of day on an invitation to avoid confusion.

9. Either the date line or the hour line should indicate whether the ceremony is to take place in the morning, afternoon or evening if the hour selected is one that would be confusing.

10. When the wedding takes place at noon, the hour may be designated as follows:

> "at high noon"
> "at twelve o'clock"
> "at twelve o'clock noon"

Reception Cards

Reception cards are enclosed in the same envelope with the wedding invitation.

It has become essential to ask for a reply on the reception card. The most commonly used forms are:

Please respond.

R.S.V.P.

The favour of a reply is requested.

Please send response to (address).

R.S.V.P. address should always be included on reception cards.

Breakfast is the word customarily used for the reception after the ceremony if it is before one o'clock in the afternoon.

Reception is the correct wording for the party after the ceremony if it is after one o'clock in the afternoon.

Typical Invitation Forms

CHURCH WEDDING

Mr. and Mrs. George Clinton Ward
request the honour of your presence
at the marriage of their daughter
Margaret Ann
to
Mr. Thomas Lothrop Denny
on Thursday, the sixth of October
at four o'clock
Wesley Memorial Chapel
Brookline, Massachusetts

Reception card to accompany invitation:

Mr. and Mrs. George Clinton Ward
request the pleasure of your company
on Thursday, the sixth of October
at half after four o'clock
Forty-eight West Drive

R.S.V.P.

Or the reception card may take this simplified form:

Reception
immediately following the ceremony
Forty-eight West Drive
Please Respond

If you are inviting a limited number of persons to the wedding ceremony and wish to have a large reception, you may use the following form, engraved on regulation size wedding paper:

Mr. and Mrs. George Clinton Ward
request the pleasure of your company
at the marriage reception of their daughter
Margaret Ann
and
Mr. Thomas Lothrop Denny
on Thursday, the sixth of October
at half after four o'clock
Forty-eight West Drive
Brookline, Massachusetts
The favour of a reply is requested

The conjunction *and* couples the names of the bride and groom-to-be. The time given is one half hour after that set for the ceremony.

To those invited to both the ceremony and reception to follow, a small card of invitation to the ceremony should be enclosed with the invitation to the reception, for example:

Ceremony
at four o'clock
Wesley Memorial Chapel

If everyone at the ceremony is to be included in the reception, the wedding invitation may read as follows, and no reception card is necessary:

Mr. and Mrs. George Clinton Ward
request the honour of your presence
at the marriage of their daughter
Margaret Ann
to
Mr. Thomas Lothrop Denny
on Thursday, the sixth of October
at four o'clock
Wesley Memorial Church
Brookline, Massachusetts
and afterwards at the reception
The Harbor Club

R.S.V.P.
48 West Drive, Brookline

CHURCH ADMISSION CARDS

Occasionally at a large wedding, cards of admittance to the church may be necessary. They usually take this form:

Please present this card at
The Wesley Memorial Chapel
Thursday, the sixth of October

PEW CARDS

Cards to reserved pews are sometimes enclosed, also, for very large church weddings.

They may be thus engraved:

Please present this to an usher
Pew No.——
on Thursday, the sixth of October

Or, the bride's mother may use her own calling card, writing in ink the number of the pew, in the upper left-hand corner; or she may write "Behind the ribbons,"

which means the holder is seated in a reserved space
marked off with ribbons.

INVITATION TO A CLUB WEDDING

Mr. and Mrs. John Charles Marshall
request the pleasure of your company
at the marriage of their niece
Rosalind Ann Richards
to
Lieutenant Julian Lee Vance
United States Navy
Wednesday, the fourth of June
at twelve o'clock noon
The Meridian Club
Evanston, Illinois

R.S.V.P.
Ten Twelve Eastdale Avenue, Evanston

This invitation is extended by the aunt and uncle of
the bride; therefore the bride's surname must be given.

The same wording is used in the home wedding invitation, *i.e.*, "request the pleasure of your company," as
it is considered the most cordial bidding in every instance where a reception follows the ceremony in home,
club or hotel.

INVITATION TO A SMALL INFORMAL WEDDING

The bride's mother may write brief notes of invitation, or she may telegraph or telephone relatives and
friends who are to be invited to a small informal wedding.

She might say to those whom she telephones:

"Kathy and Steve are planning to be married on the
sixth of June in Graceland Chapel. It is to be a small
wedding at half past four. We do want you to be there,
and also to come to our apartment following the wed-

ding for a cup of tea and some wedding cake. I hope
you can be with us."

To other friends and relatives who may live out of
town, she might write something like this:

Dear Ellen:
    Kathy and Steve are to be married at half past four
on Saturday, the sixth of June, in Graceland Chapel,
here in Huntington. It will be a small intimate wedding
with a little reception following at our apartment. You
know how much we want you to be with us on that day.

> Affectionately yours,
>
> Ruth

Informal invitations may be sent on short notice, if
unavoidable, but if possible they should be issued two
weeks in advance, the allotted time ahead for most social invitations.

If the bride's mother is not living, a close relative,
usually her aunt or grandmother, should send out the
invitations. Or the bride may write the notes herself if
she has no close relatives to sponsor her.

Following a wedding of this type, engraved announcements are customarily sent to friends and relatives who were not invited to the wedding or reception.

Invitations Keyed to Special Situations

WHEN PARENTS ARE DIVORCED

Here's where the most gracious way of coping with a
situation is the correct way. And where sensitive feelings must be handled with care.

If the bride lives with her mother who has not remarried, the following invitation is customary, using the
mother's maiden and married names, never her former
husband's Christian name:

> *Mrs. Wilson Wood*
> *requests the honour of your presence*
> *at the marriage of her daughter*
> *Alice Jane*

In the case of friendly divorce where neither parents has remarried and both expect to participate in the wedding, the bride's father and mother may be tempted to send out invitations which bear both their names as wedding sponsors, *i.e.,* "Mrs. Wilson Wood and Mr. James Lawton Wood request the honour . . . etc."

This is *not* considered good taste, however, among discerning persons and belongs only in the "raised-eyebrow department."

IF THE BRIDE'S MOTHER HAS REMARRIED

Any one of the following invitation forms is correct.

The mother alone may issue the invitation to the wedding ceremony:

> *Mrs. George Barton Bradbury*
> *requests the honour of your presence*
> *at the marriage of her daughter*
> *Alice Jane Wood*
> *to*

Or, the bride's stepfather may join his wife in sponsoring the wedding, using either of the following forms:

> *Mr. and Mrs. George Steele*
> *request the honour of your presence*
> *at the marriage of Mrs. Steele's daughter*
> *Alice Jane Wood*
> *to*

If the bride's father is more or less out of the picture:

> *Mr. and Mrs. George Steele*
> *request the honour of your presence*
> *at the marriage of their daughter*
> *Alice Jane Wood*
> *to*

Although the wedding invitation may be issued in the name of one parent alone, the reception invitation *must* be issued in the name of the couple who are giving the party. For instance, the bride's father alone may "request the honour of your presence at the marriage of his daughter." *But,* if he has remarried, he and his wife sponsor the reception and send out reception cards in both names. In the event the bride's mother has remarried, the same rule holds true for the inclusion of her husband.

Giving the bride's surname in the case of divorced and remarried parents clarifies the relationships and is customary, though not obligatory.

WHEN THE BRIDE'S MOTHER IS WIDOWED

Unless the bride's widowed mother has remarried, the wedding invitation is issued in the following form:

> *Mrs. Arthur Oliver Burton*
> *requests the honour of your presence*
> *at the marriage of her daughter*
> *Gloria Ann*
> *to*

A widower substitutes the expression "his daughter."

When the bride's mother has remarried the relationship between the bride and her stepfather is clarified thus:

> *Mr. and Mrs. James Claridge Mason*
> *request the honour of your presence*

at the marriage of Mrs. Mason's daughter
Gloria Ann Burton
to

If the bride has been adopted by her stepfather or is very close to him, the following form is correct:

Mr. and Mrs. James Claridge Mason
request the honour of your presence
at the marriage of their daughter
Gloria Ann Burton
to

WHEN A BRIDE IS BEING SPONSORED BY OTHER THAN PARENTS

The bride's surname should be given when invitations are extended by other than parents. The words "his sister," "her sister" or "their niece" are substituted for the phrase "their daughter."

If the bride is being sponsored by close friends, the invitation should carry the bride's full name, prefaced by *Miss:*

Mr. and Mrs. Paul Thomas Hale
request the honour of your presence
at the marriage of
Miss Constance Caroline Stevens
to

When a couple has no wedding sponsor, they may correctly send out their own invitations, worded as follows:

The honour of your presence
is requested at the marriage of
Miss Gertrude Jennifer
to
Mr. Benjamin Foster Decker
on Friday, the fourth of May

at four-thirty o'clock
First Presbyterian Church
Evanston, Illinois

IF IT'S ALTAR TRIP NUMBER TWO

The bride's parents should issue invitations for the second wedding of a widowed daughter just as in the first wedding. Following is the usual form:

> *Mr. and Mrs. Hamilton Trenton Burns*
> *request the honour of your presence*
> *at the marriage of their daughter*
> *Mary Lou Burford*
> *to*

The invitation for a divorced bride reads:

> *Mr. and Mrs. Hamilton Trenton Burns*
> *request the honour of your presence*
> *at the marriage of their daughter*
> *Mary Burns Burford*
> *to*

The prefix *Mrs.* is never used before the bride's name unless she and the bridegroom are issuing the invitations themselves, as in the case of the widow who has no one to sponsor her wedding:

> *The honour of your presence is requested*
> *at the marriage of*
> *Mrs. Harold White Aiken*
> *to*
> *Mr. John Patton Rusk*

The following reception card may be enclosed with the above invitation:

> *The pleasure of your company is requested*
> *Thursday the twentieth of June*

at five o'clock
The Town Club
Los Angeles, California

R.S.V.P.
33 Dalton Place

Double Weddings

A formal invitation to a double wedding of sisters is
as follows:

Mr. and Mrs. John Taranton Dexter
request the pleasure of your company
at the marriage of their daughters
Denise Leone
to
Dr. Eugene Frances Hartwell
and
Cheryl Christine
to
Mr. Jay Hornsby Alman
on the evening of Saturday, June first
at eight o'clock
Eight hundred and nine North High Street
Richmond, Virginia

When the brides in a double wedding are not sisters,
regular separate invitations may be sent by each family,
or they may unite to send the following type of invitation:

Mr. and Mrs. Richard Randell Lee
and
Mr. and Mrs. Floyd Murton Russell
request the honour of your presence
at the marriage of their daughters
Helen Tamson Lee
to
Mr. Jeoffrey Paul Herbert
and

Susan Joan Russell
to
Mr. Robert Maurice Childs

Military Weddings

The use of service titles is the only distinguishing difference between civilian and military types of formal invitations and announcements.

The groom's title (or the bride's, if she is a member of the regular armed forces) precedes his name only if he is an officer holding the rank of captain or higher in the Army, Air Force or Marine Corps, or a senior-grade lieutenant or higher, in the Navy.

Mr. and Mrs. John Edward Grant
request the honor of your presence
at the marriage of their daughter
Minerva Jane
to
Captain George Leslie Burke
Air Defense, United States Army

Only when Reserve officers are on active duty is it proper for them to use their titles on invitations and announcements.

It is more or less traditional for noncommissioned officers, privates in the Army, Air Force and Marine Corps, and petty officers and nonrated men in the Navy, to use *Mr.* before the groom's name, with the branch of corps name following on the next line, *i.e.,* "Infantry, United States Army" or "Supply Corps, United States Navy." Military men sometimes prefer the omission of the *Mr.* before the name, in which case the following is correct:

Louis Tompkins Price
Second Lieutenant, Infantry, United States Army
or:

Norman Charles Walker
Supply Corps, United States Navy

Junior officers usually prefer the omission of the *Mr.* before their names, as follows:

Claude Ruskin Wright
Ensign, United States Navy

When the groom is a member of the Reserves in active service, the correct wording on invitations or announcements would be "Army of the United States" or "United States Naval Reserve," in place of "United States Army" or "United States Navy." The preceding rules apply as to titles, etc.

If the groom is a student in a Reserve Army Officers' School, the title "Cadet" is properly used under his name and with his branch.

A formal invitation to the wedding of an Army daughter whose prospective bridegroom is in the U.S. Air Force would read:

Colonel and Mrs. Frank Carraway Morrison
request the honour of your presence
at the marriage of their daughter
Winifred June
to
Lt. Colonel George Curtis Worthington
United States Air Force

Or, if the groom is a junior officer:

to
George Curtis Worthington
Lieutenant, United States Navy

If the groom is an officer or enlisted man in the Marine Corps, the same rules apply as in the case of Army or Air Force personnel, with the designation

"United States Marine Corps" instead of "United States Army" or "United States Air Force."

Retired regular Army, Navy and Air Force officers retain their titles in civilian life usually. Their names on invitations or announcements would read:

Major General Victor Cunningham
United States Marine Corps, Retired

Retired Reserve officers, or those who are inactive, do not use their former titles either socially or in business.

ANNOUNCEMENTS

There are three choices for the opening of the announcement of your wedding:

"announce the marriage of"
"have the honour to announce"
"have the honour of announcing"

The date and year as well as the city in which the ceremony is held should be given. This holds true even after an elopement, regardless of the time that has elapsed between the marriage and the announcement.

The year and the date are always spelled out.

Although the announcements are usually issued in the name of the bride's parents, it is also permissible to issue them in the names of the bride and groom.

TYPICAL ANNOUNCEMENT FORM

Mr. and Mrs. Gordon Foster Stuart
announce the marriage of their daughter
Betsy Jane
to
Mr. Dale William Deebe
on Saturday, the ninth of February

Nineteen hundred and seventy-two
at Tabernacle Christian Church
Chicago, Illinois

"AT HOME" CARDS

Engraved "At Home" cards, such as the following, are often enclosed with announcements:

At Home
after the first of August
Thirteen hundred Elm Street
Evanston, Illinois

"At Home" cards have the advantage of informing out-of-town friends of your whereabouts. When they are not used, it is advisable for both the bride and the bridegroom to drop personal notes to those with whom they wish to keep in touch, telling their news and giving a return address.

Special Announcements

FOR DIVORCÉES

The older bride and her new husband may wish to send out announcements of their wedding—as follows:

Mrs. Stafford Williams
and
Mr. Clifford Aaron Whyte
announce their marriage
on Wednesday, the first of June
etc.

The divorcée uses her maiden name combined with the surname of her first husband. She should never call herself Mrs. George Williams, for instance, since her former husband may have married again.

If the divorced bride is still young, her parents should send out the wedding announcements as follows:

Mr. and Mrs. Burton Quincy Freeman
have the honour to announce
the marriage of their daughter
Margaret Freeman Brice
to
Mr. Jack Deeley Ford
on Saturday, the fifth of August
One thousand nine hundred and seventy-two
Washington, D. C.

A young widow's announcement would follow the example above, carrying her first husband's name (omitting her maiden name) if she wishes. The older widow, sending her own announcements, may use her husband's given name, *i.e.*:

Mrs. Harry Waldon Anderson
and
Mr. James Townsend Knight
announce their marriage

ADDRESSING INVITATIONS OR ANNOUNCEMENTS

After your lists are complete, arrange them in alphabetical order to avoid confusion in checking.

If your own family is to attend to the addressing of the invitations, enlist the aid of those who have decorative handwriting. One member of the group might be responsible for addressing all those from A to G, another from G to P, and so on. Give everybody plenty of elbow space, good pens, black ink and firm tables on which to write. The groom might like to participate in this chore if he has a steady hand.

It is important to have your lists well organized before starting on the addressing process. The complete wedding-invitation list should be broken down into three categories:

> those who are to receive invitations to the wedding ceremony only
>
> those who will receive a reception card in addition to the wedding invitation
>
> those who will receive announcements and "At Home" cards enclosed.

To compile your working list, get regular filing cards (3 by 5 inch), two sets of alphabetical indexes and two file-type boxes which will easily accommodate the number of cards you expect to have. A colored pencil may be used to initial the corner of each card in order to indicate quickly in what category it belongs: *C* for ceremony, *R* for reception, *A* for announcement.

File in alphabetical order for easy reference and to guard against confusion and needless mistakes. This is one part of wedding procedure that must be done absolutely accurately to insure everyone's receiving the proper invitation.

The second file box may be used to file alphabetically the "Acceptances" and "Regrets" as they come in, making the "count" for the caterer easily available at the appointed time.

If life is too complicated to take on this responsibility at home, stationers will refer you to a professional secretary who will relieve you of addressing, stamping and mailing your invitations. There is a charge for this service, of course.

All invitations must be sent out at one time. The invitations and enclosures are inserted in the inside envelope, which has no glue on the flap. The tissue squares which accompany the folded sheets eliminate the possibility of ink smears and should remain as the engraver has placed them.

The inner envelope should be addressed, "Mr. and Mrs. Brock," *using only the last name without address*. If it is necessary to include an entire family with one invitation, the "and family" *may* be added on the inside envelope, but it is preferable, where there are several

members of a family included, to write the individual
names on the inside envelope, like this:

> *Mr. and Mrs. Brock*
> (no Christian name)
> *Joyce and Mark*
> (if the children are under age)

In the case of families with several small children, an
invitation may bear all their names, such as, "Mary,
Jean, Jack and Fred Kingan," or you may say "The
Misses Kingan" on one invitation and "The Messrs.
Kingan" on another, and enclose these envelopes in the
outer envelope addressed to the parents.

If there is an adult son or daughter, a grandmother or
any other member in the household to be invited, that
individual must receive a separate invitation:

> *Miss Eleanor Cunningham*
> *850 Park Place*
> *New York City*

The inside envelope reads:

> *Miss Cunningham*

Two sisters living at home may receive one invita-
tion, addressed on the outside envelope to "The Misses
Gloria and Holly White," and on the inside envelope,
"The Misses White."

Two brothers (over twenty-one) receive one invitation, if they share the same address. They are addressed
as: "The Messrs. Philip and David Blake," with simply
"The Messrs. Blake" on the inside envelope.

The outside envelope bears both the name and address, with names of streets and names of states spelled
in full. No abbreviations should appear on the envelope
except *Mr.* and *Mrs.* and *Dr.*

Return Address

A return address may be written, printed or embossed on the flap of the envelope of the invitation or annoucement. This address will insure you that everyone receives the invitation or announcement.

Special Courtesies

Each member of the wedding party should receive an engraved invitation, sent at the time all other invitations are mailed.

As soon as the invitations are off the press, why not send a batch of three or four unsealed invitations on to the bridegroom's family, so that they may see them and have them as keepsakes? Your mother might enclose a little note to the bridegroom's mother, saying something like this: "Your list of invitations is ready to be sent out on such-and-such a date and we wanted you to share in the thrill of seeing them right away. . . ."

To all other members of the bridegroom's family living at their home (perhaps a grandmother or an aunt), personally addressed invitations should be sent at the regular mailing time.

Usually the minister and his wife are sent an engraved invitation to the reception at the time all invitations are mailed. However, if there is a hesitancy in not wishing to obligate the clergyman's family for a wedding gift, an informal invitation may be issued by word of mouth to the minister and his wife by the bride's mother or by the bride herself.

WHEN TO MAIL

Invitations should be mailed three weeks in advance of the ceremony; if yours is to be a very large formal wedding, you may mail them four weeks in advance.

Announcements should be mailed immediately after the ceremony, on the same day if possible. Send them only to those who were not invited to the wedding.

WHEN WEDDING INVITATIONS MUST BE RECALLED

If it is necessary to postpone or cancel a formal wedding and there is sufficient time, engraved cards, enclosed in one envelope only, may be sent to everyone who received an invitation.

Typical form for recalling invitations with reason for cancellation given:

> *Mr. and Mrs. Herbert O'Dair Gifford*
> *regret that owing to illness in the family*
> *the invitations to their daughter's wedding*
> *on Saturday, October fifteenth*
> *must be recalled*

If not wishing to state reason for recalling invitations:

> *Mr. and Mrs. Herbert O'Dair Gifford*
> *regret that they must recall*
> *the invitations to their daughter's wedding*
> *on Saturday, October fifteenth*

In case there is not sufficient time for having engraved cards made, members of the bride's family may recall the invitations verbally, by personal note, telegram or telephone.

If the wedding is definitely canceled and time permits, the bride's parents should send out an engraved card following this form:

> *Mr. and Mrs. Herbert O'Dair Gifford*
> *announce that the marriage of their daughter*
> *Frances Kay*
> *to*
> *Mr. Glen Morton Plessing*
> *will not take place*

In such circumstances wedding gifts must be returned to the senders.

CHAPTER 5 | In the Presence of This Company

It's only natural that you will want to gather your dearest friends and members of your family about you on the great day as wedding attendants. There'll be much to share that you'll all remember romantically so long as you all shall live. Give some serious thought as to whose *presence* is important to you on this momentous occasion.

"This company" will not only lend you moral support but will be highly useful and very decorative.

How many attendants you have depends on how many you want, on the size of your wedding and the place it is to be held.

In making up your list, use some discretion. Don't ask girls who can't afford to buy their own wedding attire, for it is always customary for wedding attendants to buy their own outfits, and pretty things have a way of running into money. Do try to be as considerate as possible in selecting attendants' dresses, and help them decide on a style that will be as attractive for future par-

89

ties as it is for marching to Lohengrin on the wedding day.

HOW MANY BRIDESMAIDS?

There are no cut-and-dried rules on the number you should choose. You may be married in the largest church in your town, with hundreds of guests, and yet have no bridesmaids—only a maid of honor to hold your bouquet and straighten your train as you leave the altar. Bridesmaids, like ladies in waiting, furnish the colorful backdrop to your wedding picture, so the prettier the girls, the lovelier the wedding.

Regardless of the dozen or so college friends you airily invited to be in your wedding when it was a remote subject, don't have more than eight. It always seems a bit theatrical to have a chorus looking like the Rockettes at Music Hall precede you down the aisle. For a simple wedding, you'll want fewer bridesmaids.

You may have one, two, four, six or eight. If you decide on an uneven number, you might have three bridesmaids. They will make an effective scene walking single file, followed by the maid of honor. Or you might have five, with the shortest girl leading, alone, followed by the other bridesmaids walking in pairs.

Consider yourself fortunate if the girls in your wedding party are all about the same height, so that they will make a lovely and "balanced" picture at the altar.

You will want your most intimate friends to attend you, but don't forget about the groom's sisters, if he has any.

Whether the attendants are married or not makes no difference.

MAID AND MATRON OF HONOR

Why not have both a maid and a matron of honor if you are planning a big wedding? Your married sister is the logical matron, and your unmarried sister or best friend might serve as maid.

It's going a little strong to have two matrons of honor or two maids of honor, but it may be done in a large wedding.

Your maid or matron of honor is indispensable to you at the altar. She adjusts your veil and train, she holds your bouquet during the ceremony and lifts back your face veil at the close of the ceremony. She is one of the two witnesses to sign the marriage certificate. She may help you dress for the wedding; she will see to it that the bridesmaids are ready on time and will serve as your lady in waiting in all details.

She also reminds the bride-to-be to transfer her engagement ring to her right hand, since the wedding ring must be placed *first* on her ring finger during the ceremony.

When it is time for the bridal pair to leave the reception, to dress for going away, the maid of honor helps the bride to change, and sees that the luggage is delivered to the best man. She also checks on any last-minute items.

The maid or matron of honor can be of very special assistance to the bride's mother since she, as hostess, cannot leave her guests to attend to other duties.

If it's a double-ring ceremony the maid or matron of honor carries the groom's ring to the altar, either wearing it for safe-keeping, or tying it with a tiny satin ribbon to her wrist or her bouquet.

JUNIOR BRIDESMAIDS

Is your little sister too young to be a bridesmaid . . . yet too tall to act as flower girl? By all means use her as junior bridesmaid in your wedding.

A girl of that in-between age (from a tall ten to sixteen) may lead the procession as junior bridesmaid with the bridesmaids following singly or in twos. She wears a gown similar in style to the bridesmaids' and perhaps corresponding in color to the maid or matron of honor's.

Her bouquet is of the same type as the other attendants but proportionally smaller.

The junior bridesmaid stands in the receiving line at the reception in company with the other bridesmaids.

FLOWER GIRLS

You may have two little flower girls in flowing skirts scattering rose petals in your pathway. They should be about the same size and between the ages of four and eight to be effective. Tiny tots too young to understand what is going on are likely to play games at the altar and steal the bride's show.

Little sisters of either the bride or groom may serve as flower girls, but have anyone you want. There may be one only or you may have more. They often carry Colonial bouquets or old-fashioned nosegays instead of a French basket of rose petals. Dresses may match the bridesmaids' in color, or they may be entrancing little Kate Greenaway gowns with matching bonnets. A flower girl may simply wear a pretty party dress, short length. Her shoes may be ballet slippers, in white or pastel kid.

The flower girl attends the rehearsal with her parents, but usually does not stand in the receiving line at the reception.

RING BEARER

Few brides have ring bearers any more. However, if there is a little round-eyed boy of four or five in your family, let him take part in this pageant of yours.

He should wear a white linen suit or a little-boy dark suit and white blouse (never knickers or miniature tuxedos or tails). He might carry a satin cushion with the ring tied on to insure its safe journey to the altar. It is risky to entrust the real ring to a ring bearer unless special precautions are taken.

As to his place in the processional, he may go down

the aisle with the flower girl or alone, preceding you and your father.

A ring bearer may also be a little girl, you know, and dressed much the same as a flower girl. Children look most effective when quite simply dressed.

GENERAL RESPONSIBILITIES OF THE BRIDE'S ATTENDANTS

1. Stand ready to help the bride in any way possible.
2. Entertain the bride with showers, luncheon or tea.
3. Be prompt for the wedding.
4. Be ready a half hour before time appointed for taking photographs, in order not to keep the party waiting.
5. Arrange own transportation if the bridal party is dressing at the church.
6. Give the bride a wedding gift individually, not as a group.

USHERS

The size of your wedding determines the number of ushers who will be asked to serve in the wedding. It would be ridiculous to have ten or twelve ushers at a small wedding with only a handful of guests. One usher for every twenty-five or fifty guests is considered adequate.

It is not necessary to have exactly the same number of ushers as there are bridesmaids, but the wedding party is in better balance when there is somewhere near the same number.

A large church wedding requires quite a number of ushers: at least two or more for every hundred guests invited. In a house wedding ushers are more honorary than active. It's a good idea, though, to have two who will escort each of the mothers to their respective places just before the ceremony. Also, they are helpful in seeing that very old or distinguished friends are personally taken to the reception line after the ceremony.

At the reception, the ushers do not stand in the receiving line but serve as assistant hosts.

A garden wedding may have one, two or more ushers, or you may decide on none.

When there are a number of ushers, the bridegroom usually selects one as head usher to direct the others.

They should all be dressed as nearly alike as possible. This is not only for the sake of uniformity, but it also makes them readily distinguishable from other guests.

At a formal wedding the ushers generally wear boutonnieres of white carnations with their formal clothes. Red carnations or blue bachelor's-buttons go well with the informal mood if they tie in with the general color scheme.

The ushers should arrive at the church at least an hour before the ceremony so that they may escort early arrivals to their seats.

WHO IS TO GIVE YOU AWAY?

Your father is the logical one to give you away, and he will escort you down the aisle on his right arm. If not your father, then your uncle, brother or nearest and dearest relative.

This escort is considered a member of the bridal party and should follow the dictates of the bridegroom in the matter of dress. He may use his own discretion in the selection of neckwear, but generally conforms in all other details. At the altar he stands just behind and a little to the left of the bride until the question is asked, "Who giveth this woman to be married to this man?" He then answers, "I do," and takes his place in the first pew on the left of the middle aisle, beside the bride's mother. (Or he may graciously include the bride's mother by saying, in answer to the clergyman's question, "Her mother and I do.")

If you should wish to have your mother give you away in the absence of your father, you will walk up the aisle alone. She will merely stand in her place in the front left pew, and at the proper time during the ceremony will murmur, "I do," in answer to the minister's inquiry.

THE BEST MAN

The groom usually chooses as his "chief of staff" his brother, a cousin or an intimate friend. Or the best man may be the groom's father or favorite uncle.

Except for his tie, which may vary slightly, and his boutonniere, the best man dresses exactly like the groom. (Usually he wears a white carnation or gardenia and the bridegroom wears a sprig of lily of the valley.)

The best man attends the rehearsal, sees that a head usher is appointed to direct the others, and that all are briefed on special seating arrangements for wedding guests. On the day of the wedding, he takes charge of the wedding ring (for the bride), guarding it with his very life. Often he carries a "spare" to the altar, in lieu of a slip up. If the bride is having a ring bearer, the best man helps instruct him in his duties and keeps an eagle eye on the altar proceedings, ready to give an assisting hand if the little one should falter in his (or her) duties.

The best man helps the groom pack and dress for the wedding, and accompanies him to the church a half hour before the ceremony is to take place, remaining in the vestry until the wedding march begins. He checks on the marriage license and sees that the groom has it with him before he leaves for the church.

He secures the clergyman's fee from the groom, seals it in a white envelope and hands it to the minister before or after the ceremony. He makes sure that the groom's hat and coat are taken to the vestibule of the church, with his own, before the ceremony. Afterward, it is this solid citizen who sees that the members of the wedding party leave in the proper cars, then hustles off to the reception to check on the honeymoon car, luggage, reservations, and especially to make sure that the transportation tickets are in the pocket of the groom's traveling suit.

He dances with the bride, her mother, each bridesmaid and with his own mother during the reception.

He summons the groom's parents to say good-bye to the bridal couple.

The best man is the first to toast the bride and groom at the reception, and should respond to a toast to the bridesmaids. He sees that the guest book is signed, has the groom's car ready at the right moment, and after assisting the couple in making a safe getaway, is the very last one to collapse.

CHAPTER 6 | In Holy Wedlock

Whatever your religious faith, there are certain factors to respect and consider before making your complete wedding plans.

You will not want to plan a large church wedding, for instance, during Lent or Holy Week. Lutheran and Episcopalian clergymen, as well as many others, will not solemnize a marriage service on a solemn holy day such as Christmas or Easter or any day of abstinence. Others object to Sunday weddings, largely because of the heavy church duties of that day.

As soon as your date is set and the church reserved for that particular time, you or your fiancé should get in touch with the office of the minister or priest who is to officiate at your wedding. Ask for an appointment for the two of you to meet with him for a conference.

At this preliminary meeting, basic decisions regarding the service should be made, and the organist retained. If you two are planning to have additions of your own making, as part of the marriage ceremony, they should be understood and agreed upon at this time.

97

After this session with your clergyman, you and your mother will want to have another appointment very soon. This time you should meet with the church secretary to make all the necessary wedding arrangements.

Your minister will arrange for you and your husband-to-be to have some conferences with him for serious discussions of the full meaning of marriage, its sacred and temporal aspects . . . and a full understanding of the responsibilities and obligations that a bridal couple is about to assume.

CHURCH REGULATIONS

An orthodox musical service is followed in a great number of churches. Many have a ruling that all wedding music, vocal and instrumental, must be approved by the choir director. It is usually permissible to bring a soloist from outside the church, and when a fee is paid, it is in accordance with the musician's professional rate. Soft music may be played throughout the ceremony in most churches, but during prayers the organist must remain silent.

In many churches it is mandatory that the congregation rise and remain standing during the wedding ceremony. Your minister will advise you on this important point so that your family and the groom's may set an example for guests seated in the pews behind them.

The bridal kiss at the close of the ceremony is not permitted in some churches. It is a matter of personal choice.

Members of the bridal party are not required to belong to the same church or to any church.

Ministers usually wish to have at least two other persons besides the bridal pair present for the ceremony, even though the marriage takes place in a state which requires no witnesses to the wedding.

Most Protestant churches recognize divorce and will permit remarriages to take place in the church edifice provided the couple are Christians. There are certain strictures employed in some churches, however, which may justly cause a minister to refuse to marry certain divorced couples. This should be discussed confidentially with your clergyman early in the wedding planning.

NUANCES IN WEDDING CEREMONIES

In this era of constant change in ways of living and doing, wedding ceremonies, once linked closely to age-old traditions, are assuming new aspects.

There is more flexibility within the marriage rituals. Couples are often inspired to express vocally their own heartfelt thoughts on their concepts of marriage . . . to be spoken by the bridal pair as a very meaningful addition to the wedding ceremony.

Another innovation in houses of worship is the singing of hymns by the congregation, thus giving to relatives and friends a very personal feeling of participation in the devout and happy event.

Many clergymen welcome having a member of the bride's family read well-chosen verses from the Scriptures.

Wedding music is also changing. There is more and more use of contemporary music in the church or synagogue. Brides often choose their own musical selections, subject to the approval of the clergyman and the organist.

Despite current changes, time-honored wedding traditions remain steadfast. So . . . on to a wonderful wedding of your devising, a happy blending of revered bridal customs, flavored with touches of the new

CHURCH FEES

It is well to bear in mind that there often is a very sizable fee for holding a wedding in a large city church, due to the expense of the lighting, heating and other janitorial services. Some churches require, in addition, a nominal sum for office fees, rehearsal charges and other "extras." Financial rates for church musicians are usually established by the church if regular organist and choir members are used.

If the church supplies canopy, carpet, candles, et cetera, there is an additional fee.

THE MARRIAGE CEREMONY

The modern marriage service consists of three parts *(a)* the betrothal; *(b)* exchange of vows; *(c)* the benediction. The ring ceremony is usually the most solemn part of the service, coming directly after the mutual promises of fidelity and love.

A beautiful ring ceremony, symbolizing the perfect circle of married life, is one that is used by many Protestant ministers. It is made up of the following steps:

1. The best man gives the ring to the groom
2. The groom gives it to the bride
3. The bride in turns gives it to the minister
4. The minister hands it again to the groom
5. The groom places it on the ring finger of the bride, saying (after the minister), "This ring I give thee in token and pledge of our constant faith and abiding love."

When a double ring ceremony is used, your minister will instruct you fully before the ceremony as to procedure.

CHAPTER 7 | To Be Remembered as Long as You Both Shall Live

It's time to concentrate on you . . . and that lovely gown, the costumes for your attendants and the enchantment of your wedding-party color scheme.

Bridal-gown beauty may take countless forms. It might borrow from romanticism of the past or carry out the simple lines of the present. Great masterpieces of bridal dressmaking are offered everywhere, and there is much for you to choose from in styling, fabrics, colors and designer labels.

It isn't so much the current fashion nuances you will be shopping for, as it is a once-in-a-lifetime creation for your once-in-a-lifetime walk down the aisle. And it must radiate more beauty and drama than any dress that has *ever* thrilled you.

Are you one who loves traditional things and dreams of the romance of wearing candlelight slipper satin, fashioned in princess style with portrait neckline, court train and mists of veiling, floating from a crown of orange blossoms?

Perhaps you are the type who could easily achieve an

enchanting look in a cherished bridal gown handed down in the family from bride to bride.

Or, maybe you are blessed with a slim, sleek figure that takes well to a gown in pliant silk or nylon jersey.

Would you be daring enough to wear an Hawaiian lei of white gardenias crowning your head and falling about your shoulders? Or would you consider using an exquisite, beautifully sheer sari as a flowing veil?

Perhaps you'll give up all your preconceived ideas and simply wear a beautiful borrowed dress . . . or browse about for a magnificent length of lace or a rare piece of embroidery to be fashioned into a becoming headdress.

For a garden ceremony you may decide to wear a delightfully simple white piqué dress with classic lines and carry an armful of white African daisies. Such an outfit could be bought for very little . . . or it *could* be custom-made.

Whatever your choice, there's no need to spend a king's ransom for a wedding gown. More often than not, tangible enchantment is available at a reasonable price, and brides are often on a budget.

CHOOSING YOUR WEDDING GOWN

If it's to be a formal daytime wedding, you may correctly wear a full-length gown with a sweep train, or you may prefer just a tiny train.

When a short-length dress is chosen by the bride, the entire tone of the wedding is keyed to a semiformal rather than a formal note. This type of bridal fashion is more like an exquisite afternoon dress, and may be worn with a shoulder-length veil.

The bride's attendants and the two mothers should all follow the lead of the bride, in such instances as this, and wear dresses in approximately the same short length as the bride's.

The neckline of a wedding gown should never be extremely low cut, though for evening wear at a formal affair it can be more décolleté than for daytime.

Sleeves are usually long in formal wedding gowns, with points extending over the wrists. Short, or three-quarter-length sleeves are suitable for less formal summertime weddings.

When final consideration is being given to the selection of the bridal gown, remember that back interest is very important from the wedding guests' viewpoint. Throughout the ceremony the back of the gown is all that can be seen.

When a train of considerable length is worn, it should be "bustled" for the reception, so that the bride will not be obliged to carry it over her arm whenever she moves about (cutting the cake, dancing, etc.). The alteration departments of all bridal bureaus are familiar with the process of sewing tape inside the seams of the train in strategic places, so that the train may be tied or buttoned up in a fetching bustle effect when the proper time comes. The proper time is usually before the reception line is formed, when the bride and her maid of honor go to the dressing room, and this feat is easily performed, giving the gown a charming Edwardian silhouette, floor-length all around.

Wedding Gown Colors and Fabrics

It doesn't have to be stark white. There are many flattering shades of off-white for those who feel that dead-white is unbecoming to their particular type of coloring. There's candlelight (a glowing deep-cream shade), bridal ivory, eggshell, ice-white and antique tones. An ivory shade is customarily chosen when heirloom lace is to be combined with the gown or an ancient lace veil worn. There are also pleasing pastels such as Madonna blue, blush pink, pale green and soft yellow that lend themselves to candlelight effects.

What is your most becoming color?

Whatever gown that is perfect for you can be ordered in the shade you want *if* you start in plenty of time.

There's a wide array of bridal-gown fashions and exquisite fabrics awaiting your choice. If you are planning a fall or winter wedding, lustrous satins and rich taffetas are great favorites. Peau de soie and silk-faced peau with their subdued luster are ever popular, as are floaty organzas.

Beautiful laces also are very appealing for these seasons. Picture an elegant gown made entirely of Chantilly lace with a sheer circular train bordered with more of the lace!

Designers adroitly combine bridal fabrics. Think about organza over taffeta, trimmed with re-embroidered Alençon lace, or a combination of velvet and taffeta with touches of lace. For fall or winter, bridal gowns are lavishly trimmed with crystals and pearls, tiers of ruffles, and more ruffles encircling high necklines and wrist-length sleeves.

For a mid-December wedding you would look very regal in a wedding dress of white velvet, with your attendants gowned in Christmas-red or forest-green velvet or velveteen.

Summer weddings are delightful . . . especially when held outdoors. A garden in full bloom on a summer's day would be ideal . . . or perhaps you have always hoped to be married under the huge tree on the lawn.

A charming bridal gown made in billowy organza would literally float along a garden path. Or . . . why not a voile gown, light as air, and embroidered in soft flower tones, cueing the colors of the bridesmaids' dresses?

If you should decide on an airy voile gown, why not wear a beguiling organdy picture hat with a wide, floppy brim?

Organdy for your dress, possibly with long bell-like sleeves of Chantilly lace would present a cool, composed picture of you on a mid-June wedding day. Other summery fabrics for your day of days: cotton Cluny, English net scattered with blossoms of Alençon lace, eyelet batiste, dotted Swiss, or point d'esprit.

Harmony Is the Thing

Check those notes of yours on your church or home background. (We told you they would be important.) Is there a modern feeling in the church architecture? If so, a gown of stream-lined style rather than one of the Victorian era would be most fitting. Re-evaluate the background colors before choosing your bridal colors, and make the most of whatever dramatic effects there are in the setting for your pageant.

Is your home Colonial? Then concentrate on the elegance of an Edwardian gown of lustrous satin, or a gracefully flounced dress of nylon net in period style, if you're the type to wear it.

Swiss organdy with Swiss embroidered appliqués and chapel train would be perfect in the garden.

For a summertime chapel wedding, wouldn't something light and ethereal like Chantilly lace (hand-clipped, with a delicate air) float handsomely down a white-carpeted aisle on a warm August afternoon?

An all-white Eastertime ceremony would be memorable, with the bride and at least six attendants in voluminous gowns of nylon net, walking down a church aisle bordered all the way with luxuriantly colored flowering plants . . . azaleas, tulips and hyacinths, for instance. Stabs of these same spring blossom tones would be echoed in the bridesmaids' bouquets. The bride might carry Easter lilies. The men of the wedding party would wear the correct black-and-white formal dress, whether it's a daytime or an evening affair.

What Length Train?

Bridal-gown trains usually fall into three categories, with a terminology all their own:

1. The "brush" train is the very short train that merely brushes the floor.

2. The "chapel" train is the train of medium length extending from one to three feet (as measured on

floor). It is the most popular with modern brides for all types of weddings.

3. The "cathedral" train is a long stately train (measuring up to six feet or more), suitable only for the most formal of weddings.

Most wedding-gown trains (unless they are formed by back panels) are as wide as a church aisle. They are usually mere back-line extensions of the voluminous skirts in most of today's gowns. Because of this extreme width, the trains sweep the floor most gracefully, whether they are three or six yards long.

Naturally a six-yard train belongs in a large cathedral, not in a tiny chapel or a small home or apartment. The three-yard train is a happy medium, though trains can always be cut down to conform with the type of wedding desired, without destroying the grace and symmetry of the style.

The bridal gowns for the semi-formal type of wedding are shorter-trained or completely train-less. The short (or brush) trains should sweep the floor several inches to give the most graceful look. The front hemline of all wedding gowns should merely escape the floor, to the extent that there is no danger of being tripped by the dress as you go down the aisle.

To Preserve Your Wedding Gown

An established process is now available for treating wedding gowns for long-term storage, to protect them from deterioration of every sort (discoloring, rot, insects, rust, etc.). The gown is treated and sealed in an airtight container, guaranteed to remain intact for many years. It is called the Heirloom Process; any reputable cleaner is familiar with it and can give you full details.

YOUR WEDDING VEIL

Veils are the fluff that dreams are made of. Into yours can be gathered all the romance that belongs to you on your wedding day.

Your veil may be either long or short and still be formal. The shorter lengths are more often worn by today's brides in shoulder-length, fingertip length or three-quarter length. The style of your gown and the degree of formality of your wedding should be your guide in choosing your veil. A long veil should cover the dress train, and measure at least a half-yard longer than the train when it is extended on the floor. Triple-tiered veils are flattering for tall brides.

Veils are usually fashioned of imported silk illusion, or they may be of old lace. The illusion veils are left unhemmed and may be trimmed off to any desired length. Most of them are made in circlet style, with several circles of illusion cascading around the head. The shortest circle may be thrown over the bride's headdress to cover her face, but not to extend below her bouquet in front. It is worn in the processional to the alter, never over the face as the bridal party returns up the aisle in the recessional.

In all except Jewish weddings (where it is obligatory to wear the blushing veil) a bride may follow her own preference. The maid of honor and the groom customarily assist the bride in turning back the veil immediately after the ceremony, just before the groom kisses the bride, and her face remains uncovered from then on.

Much of the beauty and becomingness of the wedding veil depend upon the style of the headdress. It forms a frame for your face and should be well suited to its contour and that of your head and coiffure.

There are endless styles in headdresses from which to choose. There are wreaths, crowns, pearl-studded caps, enchanting turbans of tulle, ruffled halos, pillboxes, off-the-face bonnets, Venise lace baby caps, Juliet caps, crisscross bands—anything your heart desires—to add that final glamour touch to your costume.

Lace is traditionally bridal, and nothing is lovelier than a veil of rare and beautiful heirloom lace, if there is such a treasure in the family. No headdress is needed with an old lace veil. It may be caught at the crown of the head with a comb, covered with fresh gardenias, sprigs of lilies of the valley, or stephanotis. Or it may be gathered into a becoming cap, fitted over a buckram shape, which is the professional way of handling fine lace.

A lace scarf might be worn in mantilla fashion, secured at the temple with a spray of tiny blossoms. Or you could have a small piece of real lace made into a baby Stuart cap, smooth over the head, or arranged in coronet style, to give you added height. An off-the-face bonnet trimmed with the lace would tie in with a Colonial-style gown, or it could be a headdress made up in Empire style to accompany a dress of that period.

It's good protection to take out a floater insurance policy on heirloom lace, covering it from the time it goes to the alteration department to be worked on until after the wedding, when your mother packs it away or has it processed with your wedding gown for safe-keeping.

Real flowers, seed pearls, tiny sequins, embroidery and narrow velvet ribbons all serve as decorative trimmings for modern headdresses, but here again, simplicity in trimmings is the best rule to follow.

Whatever your choice, be sure it is devastatingly becoming and in harmony with your gown. Also, make certain that the headdress is securely anchored with bobby pins and hair pins, so that it cannot slip when your maid of honor lifts your veil or at the reception when friends press around you.

WHAT COLOR HOSE?

Select the very sheerest of pale beige, champagne or flesh-colored hose to wear with your white or off-white wedding gown. Many manufacturers feature hose for brides, and there are exquisite lace stockings in a pale flesh-tone, beautiful with shimmering satin or any plain fabric. There are delicate blush hues, soft ivory shades . . . all appropriate for wedding wear.

WEDDING SHOES

Slippers of silk, satin or linen in a shell pump style are preferred. They should be dyed to match exactly the sample of your dress. The linens are right for wearing only with linen, piqué or other cotton fabrics.

Open-toed or open-heeled shoes are not correct. Heels should be of a comfortable height for several hours' of standing.

WILL YOU NEED GLOVES?

The answer to this question is more or less optional, depending upon the degree of formality of your wedding and your own discretion. If your wedding is formal and your sleeves are short, it seems in better taste to wear above-the-elbow kid gloves (always white, even with a pastel gown). Short kid gloves, the one-button type, are often chosen for less formal gowns or if sleeves are three-quarter length or long.

The alteration department which takes care of your dress will see to it that the third finger of the left-hand glove (your ring finger) is ripped for the occasion so that it may be tucked into the hand of your glove during the ceremony. A few stitches will repair the damage later, and your gloves will be as good as new.

In an informal wedding, when a street-length costume is worn, wear your right glove and carry the left. It eliminates fumbling at the altar when it's time to slip the ring on your hand.

Wear your engagement ring on your right hand under your glove for the ceremony, and change it back to your left hand (topping the wedding ring) before the reception.

YOUR COMPLETE WEDDING OUTFIT

Bridal gown
Wedding veil or headdress

Jewelry: simple string of pearls
tiny pearl earrings
(no bracelets)

Foundation garment

Strapless bra

Full-length slip edged with lace

Crinolines or hoops (if needed)

Note: All innerwear should be fitted with the wedding dress

Gloves

Shoes

Hoisery

Small handbag (to be left with someone in the back of church)

Fur stole or white cape (if weather is cool)

Something old, something new,

Something borrowed, something blue—and a sixpence or silver coin in your shoe.

Note: On your ride to church, remember to smooth your dress carefully under you, or lift it completely off the seat. The car should be lined with a clean white sheet to keep you spotless.

Or, if you are dressing at the church, take along a little emergency kit containing needles and thread, bobby pins, hairpins, corsage pins, cleansing tissues, scissors, Scotch tape and white chalk for covering lipstick stains. Your wedding counselor should be present, or someone with deft hands and a cool head.

IT'S TIME TO OUTFIT YOUR ATTENDANTS

Do give consideration to the dramatic little things that add another measure of charm to a wedding ceremony . . . such as dainty little flower-sprinkled parasols —for a summer ceremony, of course; or appealing wide-brimmed straw hats tied under the chin.

Or if the girls are especially young and the wedding locale is in the country, you might choose for your attendants dresses in petal-toned sheer cotton with velvet ribbons. Flower-sprigged organdy with wide taffeta sashes would be delightful . . . and organdy hats for all the girls. Then have an organdy gown yourself.

Perhaps you might have thoughts of a spring wedding, with bridesmaids in jonquil-yellow taffeta and the maid of honor in light green.

You might prefer a cherry-blossom wedding, with your bridesmaids in dotted Swiss with large butterfly bows tied in the back, carrying armfuls of cherry blossoms. What about setting the ceremony under blossoming peach trees or in a field of daisies and field flowers where a hay mower has mowed an aisle through the field, with an area for aisle, altar and guests? For such a wedding your maids might carry flowers of the field or sheaves of spring fruit blossoms. Dress them in white to match your cotton gown, tie trailing moss-green sashes around their tiny waists and let pale-pink petticoats show as they walk along the aisle.

If it's fall and you want to wear cream satin, put your bridesmaids in copper-rust or brandy-colored chiffon dresses with hats to match. Have them carry informal bouquets of yellow-gold gladioli, mounted like orchids. The maid or matron of honor might wear a dress in a shade of gold and carry deep-rust chrysanthemums. The little flower girl could wear a creamy yellow dress.

Before you go too far, consider the colors that are becoming to the various attendants. Can Betty wear yellow? Will orchids be right with Margaret's red hair?

These girls are buying their own dresses, don't forget. Be sure they are the right price for all the pocketbooks and for practical wear later. Headdresses of natural flowers or little circular veils to match each gown can be effectively concocted for a mere trifle.

As you plan, keep in mind the church or home background that is to form your setting. If there is vivid color in altar screen and windows, settle on a neutral shade and accent the costumes with flowers in all the tones of the background. If your background shades are neutral, brighten up the picture with more dashing colors. If the bride so desires, however, it is equally correct

for the attendants to wear full-length gowns when the
bride also is wearing long bridal array.

The attendants' gowns do not have to be the same
length as the bride's gown. Fairly full, short skirts covering the knee are suitable when the bridal dress is
floor-length.

It is the bride's prerogative to choose these dresses
(though the attendants customarily pay for their complete outfits.) Naturally she bears in mind both the
budget and figure problems of her attendants when she
makes her selections. It is important to the over-all effect of the wedding scene that the dresses follow the
mood set by the bride's costume, but the simpler the design of the attendants' outfits, the smarter the wedding
and the more practical for later wear.

Most brides find that greater symmetry of color is
achieved by choosing bridesmaids' dresses all in the
same color tones, as well as in matching styles. The
honor attendant may then wear the same style, or a similar design, in the same or a harmonizing color.

If you have your heart set on having a "shaded" wedding party, with dresses ranging from a light shade of
blue, for instance, on into a deep, deep tone for bridesmaids, seek the advice of an expert bridal counselor in
working out these details. Often the effect of these different tones of the same color is not entirely pleasing in
artificial light or in candleglow, and the attendants cannot always be positioned advantageously in their relationship to each other. Just as in a "rainbow" type wedding, where many different pastel tones are worn, the
final results may appear mottled and ineffective if a
practiced hand is not available to help work out the
details.

Junior bridesmaids' and flower girls' dresses should
conform in mood to the others in the wedding party, but
should be kept suitable to their ages and in correct proportion to their measurements.

Sleeves may be short, three-quarter length, or long.
Shoulders are always covered in the church ceremony,
and necklines conservative, never extremely low-cut ei-

ther in back or front. As with the bridal gown, it is well to remember that back interest in the attendants' gowns will add to the beauty of the altar scene.

Fabrics

Peau de soie, crepes, point d'esprit, taffeta, matte jersey and faille are on the year-round list for bridal party dresses.

If you are planning a summer wedding, the choice of fabrics for bridesmaids' dresses is wide and very appealing. Very lightweight fabrics are a must for a summer day that could be sizzling.

These featherweight materials will be cool, comfortable and fresh-looking throughout the wedding day. There's a variety of voiles, some with soft flower prints or embroidered motifs, also organdies, batistes, dotted Swiss, chiffon and point d'esprit.

When you confer with your bridal counselor, she will guide you wisely on the dress selection for your attendants, and see to it that the style you choose relates to your wedding gown.

For a fall or winter wedding, velvet or velveteen (probably the latter, less costly) is very effective in rich fall colors that would provide a lovely background for your gown in satin, taffeta, faille, peau de soie or lace.

The bridal attendants' dress-fittings should be carefully arranged, with someone in attendance who will follow through on all the small details. If cocktail-length dresses are the order of the day, all lengths should conform with each other. (Skirts of this type usually measure about thirteen inches from the floor.) If the dresses are long, with slight trains, they should all be altered to brush the floor in conformity. This is one time in your life when it pays to be fussy about the fit and finish of garments to be worn on parade. All petticoats or slips for attendants should be of equal fullness or, if hoops or crinolines, the same size.

Headdresses

Headdresses conform in style to the type of gowns worn and to the bride's own headdress. Try to settle on a style that will be as becoming as possible to all the girls. There are myriads of trifles on the market, such as tulle circlets with flower topknots, half-hats of fabric to match the dresses, velvet headbands, Juliet caps of taffeta or velvet strips, coronets and off-the-face bonnet types.

Many of the dresses available in bridal shops come with especially designed hats or headdresses made along these lines, so inquire about them when you are dress-shopping.

Fresh flowers worn in the hair can be effective when they match the bridesmaids' bouquets. There are nosegays with ribbon streamers, halos, bandeaus of blossoms, dainty wreaths, garlands and rosettes—any number of countless concoctions that you and a clever florist can devise. The bill for these should be included in the bride's over-all floral statement, not charged individually to each attendant.

More headdress ideas: Crisp flat bows, garlands of real flowers that fall to the shoulders, wide organdy hats with wavy brims, big floppy straw hats.

Gloves and Shoes

It is the bride's responsibility to decide whether the bridesmaids should wear gloves or not. If the bride wears long gloves with a short-sleeved bridal gown, then it is important that the attendants wear gloves of some sort. For a formal evening wedding, when the maids are wearing short sleeves, above-elbow-length white kid gloves are most appropriate. Short white kid gloves with one button may be worn in the less formal daytime affairs. Kid gloves should always be white for a wedding.

In summertime ceremonies, gloves for the bridesmaids and maid of honor are often omitted unless it is a highly formal occasion.

Gloves are left on during the reception until the refreshments are served.

Shoes of shell pump style, dyed to match the dresses, are in order for the bridal attendants. Open-toed sandals are not acceptable for wedding wear.

Note: Hose and shoe colors of the complete wedding party should all conform. This is true also of make-up and nail polish which should be in the same blending tone.

Be sure your attendants aren't planning to wear jangling bracelets with their wedding togs . . . or ill-assorted earrings and other jewelry. It's a happy solution to the jewelry problem if you present them with something suitable to wear for the occasion.

THE MOTHERS' COSTUMES

Next to you and your bridal party, your mother is more important than anyone. As hostess and "ambassadress" she should be dressed to express beauty and graciousness.

Everyone will be looking at your mother and the groom's mother, and both should be gowned in harmony with your wedding colors. They will stand together in the receiving line and should complement each other in the shades they choose. The formality of the wedding, of course, will dictate the type of dress. Whatever it is, it should bespeak quiet assurance and poise.

Cardinal principles to follow in selecting a dress are that it should be soft of hue (violent contrasts make the figure look heavy) and flawless in line. Pale shades such as muted blue or green, champagne-beige and gray are all recommended colors. The glowing purples, wines and rosy shades are splendid tonics for graying hair, and bring a glow to the tones as well.

It's better to choose a dress of understated elegance than to be overdressed. An exquisitely simple dress needs only some beautiful jewelry.

For Daytime Formal Weddings

Either cocktail-length or full-length dresses for the mothers are correct in daytime formal weddings, regardless of the gown-lengths worn by the bridal attendants. The bride's mother has the privilege of making this selection and following through to see that the dresses of both mothers conform in type and length.

If the bride and all her attendants are wearing short-length dresses, the mothers wear the same short length. But when the bride has chosen a long wedding gown, even though her attendants are in shorter lengths, the mothers may correctly choose long dresses if they wish. It stands to reason that there should be complete conformity among the principals when the bride and her bridal party are all in short-length dresses; or if all should wear long gowns, again the mothers would follow suit.

The mothers generally wear hats or headdresses of some sort for all church ceremonies. White kid gloves are a necessary part of each mother's costume, also, at a formal wedding. When sleeves are short, above-elbow length white kid are correct.

Club and hotel weddings customarily require the same dress regulations. When a wedding is in the home of the bride and the mother is the hostess, hats are not obligatory for either mother. When they are worn, they should be an alluring part of the mothers' costumes, either matching their individual dresses or complementing them in color. The concoctions may be mere wisps of draped tulle, velvet, chiffon or any fabrics which match the gowns. Or the hats may be large dressy straw shapes, or diminutive ones. When flower trimmings are chosen, consideration should be given to the flower corsages which are traditionally a part of the mothers' accessories, lest these elements vie with each other.

Orchids are the favorites of most mothers, with the delicately toned blossoms favored over the deep purple ones. Corsages, of course, are always worn with the stems pinned downward, just as the flowers grow. A small nosegay is effective pinned to a little velvet or silk faille purse, or to a sable or mink scarf.

For Evening Formal Weddings

A formal evening wedding may be more dressy than a daytime wedding. The mothers may be as formally gowned as they wish to be, but if their gowns are at all décolleté, they should wear a covering over their shoulders for the ceremony. They may wear dressy afternoon dresses; or they could choose floor-length dinner gowns, with covered shoulders.

An adornment of fresh flowers may be worn in the hair. Or a mere hint of a headdress will serve as head covering. Orchid corsages are considered the most flattering for formal wear.

Gloves are worn by both mothers through the ceremony and in the receiving line. White or off-white kid gloves are correct for formal occasions.

Short white kid gloves (wrist-length) are appropriate when sleeves are long or three-quarter length. Three-quarter length gloves are not worn for formal dress, though the wrist-length "shorties" can be worn with even the shortest sleeve.

CHAPTER 8 | Rose Petals
In Your Pathway

Whatever type of wedding you are having and whatever its locale, the right flowers will set it off to perfection. An ingenious florist often can create a fairyland effect with a handful of blossoms against a backdrop of greens at the altar . . . or add downright drama to a muted attendant's gown by spiking her bouquet with vivid color in just the right proportions. So select your florist carefully and start working with her in your early planning stages.

In this age of specialists, you'll be wise to choose a florist who has a reputation for being outstanding in wedding décor. The church secretary is usually well informed about florists who have successfully decorated the church under consideration. She will be glad to help you. Or you may wish to ask your bridal counselor for the names of several wedding florists.

Before deciding on your wedding colors, meet your florist at the church or wherever the wedding is to take place. Carefully consider the interior color scheme, the layout and architectural effects. You may want to plan

118

on having flowers that are in season in order to hold expenses down. Or, again, you may have a desire to go all out and splurge on sprays of fresh orange blossoms sent refrigerated from California, or to import leis of orchids and exotic tropical greens from Hawaii. Whatever your dream, this is the time to talk it over with an expert and get estimates on costs right at the start.

CHURCH DECORATIONS

Simplicity of effect in altar decorations is considered the best taste. It is preferable to underdecorate the church rather than to overdecorate it. In some churches there are rules prohibiting the use of flowers or greenery of any sort. In others, white flowers may be used, but colored blossoms are not permitted. The church secretary should be consulted regarding the church rules for decoration if your florist is not fully informed on this point.

White flowers and greenery are used more than any other decorative effects at the altar. Often there is only one large arrangement of white flowers, or perhaps two altar vases, backgrounded with greens and lighted candelabra in the chancel of the church.

There are greens of many varieties that lend themselves well to this sort of decorating. Among them are palms and ferns, boxwood and evergreens, and such beautiful leaves as magnolia, lemon, huckleberry, rhododendron, eucalyptus and croton.

Flowers for the church or synagogue also include a wide range for selection, dependent upon the season and suitability to the wedding décor. You can choose anything from white roses, tulips, lilacs, lilies, daisies, stocks, snapdragons, peonies, gladioli to chrysanthemums, asters, dahlias, carnations, shaggy fujis and poinsettias. If it is to be a pastel-toned wedding in the spring or summer (and if the church will permit color), you may want to fill altar containers with flowering branches of apple or cherry blossoms, pink dogwood, yellow mimosa, or blue delphinium. White lilacs are lovely for Eastertime, and white poinsettias for Christmas weddings. Naturally, it isn't the quality of flowers and greenery that should be considered, but the artistry and originality employed in their use.

Candles are flattering in their effect, and may be used for late afternoon and evening ceremonies. There are tall single standards, those of cathedral type or the many-branched candelabra. Aisle-post candles are entrancing when an all-out candlelight wedding is planned. And don't overlook the idea of massing small flickering candles on low window sills of the church wherever possible, and match them with tall tapers mixed with greenery at the altar. White tapers are customary in decorations unless you are carrying out the delicacy of blush pink or pale blue in your bridal costumes and want candles in a pastel tone to match.

Markers are usually placed on every second or third pew, extending from the front of the church to the middle section or thereabouts. These markers should be of fairly small proportions and in conformity with the rest of the flowers; never so massive that they extend noticeably into the aisle or hamper guests from having easy access to the pews. Most tasteful are miniature bouquets of the same type flowers carried by the bridesmaids, or sprigs of lilies of the valley backed by their own green foliage, to match the flowers in the bride's bouquet or the bridegroom's boutonniere.

When you are conferring with your florist at the church, you might well have a look at the pedestals, urns, vases and baskets which are available there as flower containers. It is a good time also to check with the florist on whether to use an aisle carpet that is put down in advance of the wedding, or the "pull-back" canvas which the ushers stretch to the back of the church just before the organ strains of the "Bridal Chorus" begin. When the aisle carpet is laid in advance of the wedding, it is usually tacked down on the edges and is often more even in its effect than when put down by the ushers. Ushers seat guests from the side aisles in this case, and white ribbons must be placed across the tops of the pews and extending across the center aisles to block anyone from entering there. Some prefer this method for safety and for expediting the wedding procedure.

For a Springtime Wedding

Quince, plum or wild cherry blossoms spilling over from tall altar vases and tied in tiny bunches at pew ends are effective in a church wedding. Though white flowers are traditional for altar embellishment, you might consider introducing a spot of color to add a note of sunny springtime, if church rules permit. Combine Easter lilies with yellow forsythia branches, if yellow is one of the bridal colors. Easter lilies combine well with shiny lemon leaves in altar bouquets and for aisle-post decorations. Or, what about an arrangement of potted tulips or jonquils, interspersed with potted ferns on either side of the chancel?

Lilacs in lavish bunches lend themselves exquisitely to springtime weddings. And geraniums are not to be overlooked either. Just picture a bride carrying white geraniums in a closely formed cluster, surrounded by attendants carrying shower bouquets of ivy spiked with coral geraniums. To complete the picture, potted coral and white geraniums would decorate the altar rail, with bouquets of white stock against a background of green in the chancel.

Short-stemmed flowers massed in low bunches could be used as chancel decoration in a small church. Try fragrant lilies of the valley mixed with white violets, and baby's breath as pew markers and *prie-dieu* decorations. Bows of white tulle tied to the bouquets would give an airy, ethereal effect.

Is It to Be a Summertime Ceremony?

Roses and the June bride go together as naturally as cake and its frosting. Creamy white roses are old-fashioned favorites though there are many gorgeous varieties of white roses, ranging in shade from snow-white to deep, deep cream color. When roses are chosen for altar decoration, the bride and her attendants could follow the same theme by carrying dainty arrangements of sweetheart roses, stephanotis and forget-me-nots entwined with ivy clusters.

Peonies, snapdragons, snowballs and spirea are effective summer flowers that fall into easy and graceful arrangements. Night-blooming stock and white larkspur are appropriate for chancel ornamentation, as are white albion lilacs. Masses of field daisies create a memorable wedding picture when used in the large altar vases and echoed throughout the church in smaller motifs, on window ledges and tied as nosegays for pew markers.

Ropes of mixed summer blossoms, in light pastel shades, would add a new note, stretched along the main-aisle pews in place of the usual white ribbons. To continue the theme, use the same flowers in large clusters at the chancel, and have small bunches of them arranged as markers for the pews.

At one lovely wedding the bride in white satin carried a bouquet of white heather mixed with lilies of the valley. Her attendants, also in white, were breath-taking as they walked down the aisle carrying red roses artfully arranged with sprigs of the feathery white heather. The continuity was carried out at the altar, where bouquets of white roses were mixed with white heather and set off by soft green foliage in large handsomely shaped urns.

At another formal church ceremony, in which the bride wore an old-fashioned blue gown, the altar and pews were decorated in a Madonna color scheme, with blue and white delphiniums and gladioli arranged in Colonial style bouquets. The same arrangement, in miniature, was reflected in the flowers carried by the bride and her attendants.

Pastel-toned snapdragons arranged in fanned-out shapes in large containers at the altar are impressively lovely when matched in mood by a bridal party carrying snapdragons of more vivid shades. Vases of trailing white-edged ivy can be artistically adapted to church decorations also, and repeated in theme by having the bridesmaids wear pretty little crowns of the small-leafed ivy in their hair.

When a large church is used for a small wedding, it may be attractively decorated to resemble a chapel by screening off the back section with boughs of greenery, birch branches or a trellis of rambler roses or thick-growing vines.

For an Autumn Wedding

Autumn, with its rich vibrant colors, presents striking possibilities for contrasts at the altar. Imagine a chancel aglow with amber-toned chrysanthemums in lovely basket containers, softly lighted by white candles in tall candelabra, wound with trailing greens and more mums. Then, think of having the bridal attendants in tawny copper shades of velvet, walking to the altar carrying candles entwined with flowers and autumn leaves—and prepare for a wedding scene of incredible beauty.

Spider mums and shaggy-petaled fujis are in season from the first of September until Christmastime, and may be found in orchid tones, bronze, white and yellow. Mixed with croton leaves, they are most unusual and charming for bouquets as well as for altar decoration.

White asters mixed lightly with spears of wheat or rye, barely or oats, provide a beauteous chancel background for rich jewel-toned gowns.

When Renaissance colors are chosen for bridesmaids, reflecting the beauty of the stained-glass cathedral windows, consider for the altar effects a large center container filled with calledian leaves and huge dahlias of autumn tones mixed with white flowers. And have the maids carry leaf bouquets of calledian leaves with floral pendants.

For a Thanksgiving wedding, choose grape tones for the bridal attendants (in taffeta or moire) with pale-pink dahlia or aster bouquets arranged in garlands to fall to the hemlines of their dresses. You, as the bride, might wear pale shell-pink satin and carry pale-pink-throated orchids surrounded by pink asters. The church decorations might consist of altar vases filled with pink dahlias and snapdragons against deep-green foliage. On the reception table clusters of deep-purple grapes falling from a center bowl of pink flowers would be magnificent. And, of course, serve pink champagne.

A Winter Wedding

Roses and carnations are the best-in-season flowers for winter wedding decorations. Many unusual effects can be achieved with the use of winter greens as background arrangements.

An all-white wedding, with the attendants carrying red roses, would be stunning silhouetted against deep-green boxwood decorations in the chancel and white roses in vases placed artistically at the altar.

Had you thought of a winter wedding to take place in complete candlelight, with tapers of various sizes flickering from all parts of the church?

Azaleas in potted form may be found at most florists along toward the end of winter. Gorgeous in their delicate beauty, they might be used for altar decorations in pure white or a pale pink. Geraniums in the same color might be considered also at this time of year.

FLOWERS FOR A HOME WEDDING

The altar may be banked with greenery and a container of flowers placed on each side, possibly with candelabra in the background. Or you might use small white pillars (available at most florists) to hold vases of flowers and trailing ivy.

Sometimes pedestals or tall containers overflowing with blossoms are used to indicate the aisle along which the bridal party enters. But don't attempt to make a home wedding too formalized. A nice idea for forming an aisleway to the altar is to have the bridesmaids carry a rope of greenery, with flowers tucked in here and there. The rope is held a little above fingertip length by attendants, who stand evenly spaced on each side of the aisleway until the bride reaches the altar. The maids then gather the rope of flowers into looplike folds and walk, two by two, to their places at the altar.

The stairway and hall banisters in a home wedding may be lightly festooned with greenery and nosegays, and the house very simply decorated with vases of mixed flowers.

If only the reception is to take place in your home, the background for the receiving line is your main decorating concern. One wedding reception was planned so that the end of the living room served as the background for the receiving line. Tall French windows, directly behind the receiving group, were hung with flower ropes, and directly over the bride and groom in the receiving bower hung an old English "kissing loop," wound with myrtle.

If you'll be satisfied with something a bit less ornate, then decorate the fireplace mantel with greenery and a low arrangement of flowers to extend all the way across. Have lighted candles in holders at each end if the hour is suitable, for there is a special dignity and charm in the soft glow of candlelight. Or let your receiving line background remain unadorned, and mark the spot only with pedestals containing flower arrangements.

A GARDEN WEDDING

You'll want to keep the decorations for a garden wedding as natural as possible. A flower-bordered pathway to the altar would be the most appropriate, with a lovely green-grass walkway, not covered by white canvas if your gown has no train.

The altar spot should be carefully chosen so that guests may easily see the service. It may be in an open summerhouse, situated on a high vantage point. Or it may be near a semicircle of bushes, which would serve as the background.

Pedestals holding arrangements of garden flowers might be placed on each side of the garden altar-place, if you like. But unless this is a highly formal affair, keep it charmingly simple, with only real outdoors effects.

FLOWERS FOR THE RECEPTION TABLES

If it's to be a big formal wedding, you will want to confer with the caterers about available table coverings before you settle on any of the flower decorations for the reception. If you are having a large buffet table with many small guest tables, it is likely you will hold to white for your linens. Pale blue or pink table cloths would be very pleasing too, if the caterer is so equipped.

Traditionally, white flowers on spotless white linen, with gleaming silver appointments and flickering candlelight, always present a picture of loveliness.

Bowls overflowing with white roses, gardenias or lilacs would be appropriate to use as centerpieces, with lighted candles in silver candelabra on either side. For the small guest tables, silver or crystal baskets of miniature size, filled with lilies of the valley, freesias or stephanotis would be tasteful touches. Or, for a sit-down breakfast, you might prefer small bowls of flowers for each of the small tables.

Bridal colors of French blue and gold served as the keynote to one very pretty buffet table, planned by an autumn bride who wanted something different and gala for her most memorable party. A large round table was contrived by placing a sixty-inch table top over a small sturdy table, and a knife-pleated, two-tiered cloth of silky gauze was made for it in soft shades of blue. A wide French blue velvet ribbon added its finishing touch, encircling the edge of the table and ending in a tailored bow with streamers to the floor. The table centerpiece was the main attraction—a large white epergne overflowing with beautiful yellow roses and flanked by tall flickering candles. A two-tiered bride's cake made in heart shape was topped with a little heart-shaped nosegay of yellow and white flowers. Festooning the cake were individual corsages of yellow roses, button mums and freesias.

Another decorative idea which created favorable comment at a small informal reception during the Christmas holidays echoed the theme of the double-ring ceremony. Two large rings were fashioned of leaves sprayed with white and intertwined, then laced with stephanotis, frothy baby's breath and sparked with deep-red carnations. These wreaths were hung like inter-twined rings in the center of the plain-toned wall just behind the buffet table. A towering bride's cake was en-circled with sprigs and blossoms to match the flower rings on the wall and became the focal point of a distin-guished white and gold reception table.

You might have a trio of round tables, arranged to-gether in an artistic group, rather than just one table, if your dining room is large enough to accommodate them. The tables would all be covered with circular cloths reaching to the floor. Festoons of ivy leaves and flowers would be effective garlanded like swags on the front of each table. One table could be for tea and cof-fee, another for champagne, and the center one for dainty sandwiches and the bride's cake. Colorado car-nations and baby calla lilies would be unusual for dec-orating the cake table, and also the cake itself. Or you might have parrot tulips, shading from deep pink to del-icate orchid. And have the florist turn the petals back, so that the stamens show and the flowers take on a lotus-like effect.

As an unforgettable centerpiece for the bridal table you may wish to have your attendants place their bou-quets right down the center of the table when they come into the dining room.

Make sure, when you are planning reception details, to have at the bride's table two toasting glasses tied to-gether with white ribbon and a tiny nosegay of lilies of the valley. After the cake-cutting ceremony you and your groom will want to drink the first toast together (as Mr. and Mrs.)—so do it gaily with champagne glasses tied romantically together, for all to see.

YOUR BRIDAL BOUQUET

Yes, the bridegroom buys it, that's true. But you should have an active part in its selection, so that your flowers will conform perfectly to the wedding motif.

White orchids seem to be the most cherished by brides everywhere. Lilies of the valley have become known as the bride's flowers.

Velvety white roses are choice flowers for bridal bouquets, as are stephanotis blossoms, those waxy star-shaped flowers which look very much like orange blossoms. There are stately lilies; round compact bouquets of narcissi, sweet peas, and white violets; or arm bouquets of lilacs, chrysanthemums or tulips. Against a background of greenery at the altar, a cascade bouquet would be effective with flowers extending all the way to the hemline of your gown (gardenias, perhaps, with trailing greens; or beautiful long-stemmed roses with their own foliage).

Consider a spray of butterfly orchids, or lilies, or of lilacs attached to your prayer book. Or how about a cluster of white freesias set in the center of a soft bow of white tulle? Perhaps you will want your florist to make you a dainty fan, dotted with delicate blossoms.

Bouquets can be made on a handle or cuff which you can slip over your arm and later easily transfer to the maid of honor at the altar.

Many bridal arrangements are fashioned with an orchid center that can be slipped out and used later as a going-away corsage.

CORSAGES FOR INFORMAL WEDDINGS

Shoulder corsages are most generally worn with informal dress. But if it suits your costume, you may wear a wristlet of tiny asters or small blossomed flowers . . . or carry a few single stalks of long-stemmed chrysanthemums.

Orchids of rare species and colors combine beautifully with more tailored street costumes and are lovely on furs. Rubrum lilies offer a dash of bright hue for dark-colored things. Camellia foliage combined with carnations make a pretty bouquet; and often variegated foliages can be put to use without the benefit of blossoms when in the hands of an ingenious florist.

If you have a yen for all white flowers in your corsage, you might like lilies of the valley with a gardenia center, or all white violets.

Pin the stems of the corsage flowers downward, just as they grow naturally, and you can enjoy their fragrance more.

BRIDESMAIDS' BOUQUETS

When you settled on those lovely gowns for the attendants, couldn't you just picture them as a background for the flowers?

You probably thought then and there, roses and anemones will set them off to perfection. . . . Or maybe: Shaggy pink fujis will carry out the color blends best. But whatever you've decided on, we've only a little word to add. Don't let the size of the bouquets overpower the girls or cover up their dresses. Tremendously large bouquets are not smart.

These flowers may be in sprays or in round and formal bouquets. They may be in a Colonial arrangement. They may be flower muffs, nosegays adorning artistic little fans, ropes or garlands, flower-covered parasols, armfuls of blossoms or baskets spilling over with vibrant color.

For a morning wedding, how would you like your attendants to carry prayer books with white-edged trailing ivy, or a simple arrangement of blossoms framed with begonia leaves?

Are you familiar with "glamellias"? They are gladioli which have been artistically wired, blossom by blossom, to resemble camellias. Made up in variegated array, they will be conversation pieces that add exciting colorful touches to your wedding.

Take the samples of all dress materials to the florist to work out color effects. If you are having a period wedding, by all means have your florist arrange to see the gowns so that the bouquets will fit into the picture perfectly.

Check with your florist on all other details such as:

Prayers bench

Candelabra

Tapers

Canvas

Canopy

Corsage for organist (if she is a special friend).

CHAPTER 9 | **To Love and to Treasure**

Your shopping time-table now brings you face to face with the thrilling prospect of selecting those cherished patterns for your household trousseau. No treasure-hunt that you will ever experience in your whole life can possibly mean more to the two of you than this exciting safari into the stores, which you are about to make.

Whether you plan, by choice or circumstance, to live in a furnished apartment or to have a home of your very own, you will want to invest in table-setting pieces that will give you a glow of happiness and pride in their ownership.

"Good design" is the basic premise on which you'll doubtless make your selections. This means quality workmanship, pleasing lines and lasting value guaranteed, and has nothing to do with whether or not the item is contemporary or traditional in style. Choosing what appeals to you and having it speak out clearly to you as your choice of all choices is one of the foremost factors that should influence you on deciding on your individual

131

silver, china and glassware patterns—and in ordering your linens.

Many of the things you buy now will grow lovelier and more precious as the years go by. So shop wisely and thoughtfully. Confer with your groom on the big decisions and make certain before you sign up for any single piece—that you'll love and cherish it "from this day forth."

THE BRIDAL REGISTRY

Before you embark on the happy task of choosing treasures for your future home . . . your silver, china, crystal, glassware, etc., be sure to visit the Bridal Registry of a leading department store *and* a shop that specializes in gifts for the home.

Go with a list of the gifts you would like to receive, and turn it over to the Registry. It is up to you to advise your friends about the stores where you have listed your gift preferences.

It's best to register your list before sending out those wedding invitations. In the meantime you and your husband-to-be will resolve those important decisions on the patterns in silver, china and glassware you have chosen.

LINENS

Look for established brand names backed up by the most reputable firms. Avoid imitations. Look for a "No Weighting" marking on labels to insure that no overdose of starch or sizing has been used. To determine this, rub parts of the fabric together over a dark surface. If a white powdery substance appears, it indicates that the item is sized. If heavily sized, the fabric will be sleazy after the first washing, when the sizing is removed.

Your Bedroom Linens

Contour sheets that are made in the blended fabrics of polyester and cotton are at the head of the bed-linen list. Their no-iron aptitude is a great boon.

Sheets and pillowcases in muslin and percale are of course lower in price. They come in various grades of fabrics and the service they give will depend on the quality you select.

The closeness of weave in relation to the thread count, and the strength of yarns are important to consider. The best-quality fabrics are soft and smooth as silk to the touch.

Percale is a great favorite, being of smooth texture, soft and lightweight. The thread count in a percale sheet begins at 180 per square inch, with the finest grade having 200 or more. Percale sheets cost less to launder when laundry is paid for by the pound, and they are lighter to handle.

Muslin sheets are not as expensive as percale but are rougher to the touch. They wear well and stand up to commercial laundering better than anything else, though they are bulky to handle. The quality of muslin may be coarse or fine, depending on the size, texture and number of yarns in the fabric.

A solid hem on both sheets and pillow cases is more practical than a hem-stitched one. Machine-made monograms are available for much less than hand-embroidered ones of course. Your linen shop will have many examples of monograms to show you, and will gladly advise on them.

Examine sheets carefully before you buy, checking for firmness of weave, strong tape selvage, small, even stitching and straight hems, closed at the ends.

Blankets

Thermal-weave blankets are very light in weight, with open, airy textures almost like crochet. They are available in wool, acrylics and polyesters. A sheet or other light covering *must* be used over this type of blanket to retain body heat.

Conventional blankets do of course come in a wide range of natural and man-made fibers. There are many variations in grade and texture, but the best quality is the best buy. Look especially for softness, resilience, close weave, deep nap, and check on washability. If you prefer an electric blanket, choose a reliable, guaranteed brand and buy it from a reputable house. One electric blanket will take the place of a summer blanket or two winter blankets. In double-bed sizes dual controls are available.

Minimum Requirements for Bed Linens

A satisfactory sheet supply for a beginning home-maker can be figured on the basis of six sheets for each bed. This allows for two sheets in use, two sheets in the laundry and two in reserve. Pillow cases should be figured on the basis of three cases for each pillow.

Here are minimum requirements in basic items:

12 sheets for twin beds	2 summer blankets per bed
6 sheets for double bed	1 mattress pad per bed
6 pillow cases	1 mattress cover per bed
2 pillows	1 blanket cover per bed

2 winter blankets per bed, or 1 comforter per bed, or 1 electric blanket per bed
1 bedspread per bed

Bathroom Linens

Bath towels should be highly absorbent and able to withstand tugging and twisting. Good absorbency is assured when the well-bleached cotton yarn is soft, evenly spun and of deep pile. The underweave of a terry towel is the best indicator of its wearing qualities. The lengthwise and crosswise threads should be firm, close and tightly woven. In the best-quality towels you will find the surface loops (which act as small sponges) closely spaced to absorb adequately the moisture. To check uniformity and tightness of weave, hold the towel up to the light. If only tiny pinholes of light show through, it has passed the test. Selvages should be fast-woven, hemmed or overstitched for durable wear. Hems should also be inspected to see that they are sewn with small close stitches, with overstitching at the corners.

Most brides order their towels in matched sets, consisting of bath towel, face-hand towel, washcloth and bath mat. These usually match in color and design and customarily are monogrammed with three initials. Care should be used not to overdo the number of monograms displayed in a bathroom. When the towels are all in matching monogram design, it is better to omit monograms on bath mat and shower curtain.

Guest towels made of terry are by far the preferred type. They come in a delightful variety of floral patterns, stripes, modern motifs and soft or rich colors.

The following list should be adequate as a starter for a family of two with one bathroom to equip. One-half this amount will serve for each additional bathroom, as a minimum.

For your bathroom

12 large bath towels	6 guest towels
12 small towels	2 bath mats
6 washcloths	2 bathroom rugs
6 hand towels	1 shower curtain

Kitchen Linens

Dish towels of modern design can add great individuality and perkiness to a kitchen. Artfully designed tea towels may be used as place mats, and colorful kitchen café curtains may be made of gay linen towels.

You'll find that good quality muslin, linen and terry towels in bright prints are the most practical for drying glass, china and silver. There are large-size dish towels adaptable to pots and pans, and other large pieces. When buying, avoid fuzzy yarns, as they tend to leave lint and streaks. For general purposes a coarse open-weave is the most absorbent, and a guaranteed colorfast fabric, the most enduring.

Here are the minimum requirements:

1 dozen dish towels
6 dish cloths
6 pot holders
  miscellaneous cleaning cloths
  Paper towels in a dispenser should be included in the modern kitchen.

Table Linens

The type of life you plan to lead and the amount of space you have should determine the quantity of your table linens. If, like most young-marrieds of today, you will be following the trend toward informal entertaining, concentrate mainly on place mats of attractive variety and a goodly supply of the small gay table cloths available in so many pleasing shapes, textures and designs.

With your china as your guide, experiment freely with colors for your informal dining. Insist on good workmanship, colorfastness, straight hems and neat stitching in your table linen selections.

For formal entertaining, you'll want the very loveliest linen you can buy. It may consist of no more than a dozen fine linen tea napkins to start with, or a charming white organdy or pale damask dinner cloth to set off your new china. If you are uncertain about your china colors, select white or off-white linens and play safe.

Here is a minimum list:

1 dinner cloth of linen, organdy, damask or lace with 12 matching napkins (cloth of correct size for table, as measured with and without leaves; round cloth for round table)
2 sets of plastic place mats with 8 napkins
2 place mat sets for luncheon and dinner, with appropriate napkins
1 formal place mat set of embroidered linen and 8 matching napkins
1 dozen cocktail napkins of linen

SELECTING YOUR DINNERWARE

The china patterns you select may easily be the keynote to your entire table-setting coordination. To shop wisely, you will want to learn all you can about the general subject in order to judge the specific items intelligently.

China is a broad word used almost generally today for every type of dinnerware. Originally it meant the fine translucent porcelain produced by the Chinese in the sixth century. Called "Chinaware" by the English, the name was later shortened to the common noun "china." And now stores have their "china sections," which include everything from coarse pottery pieces to the most expensive gold-encrusted dinnerware sets.

Fine China, Earthenware and Pottery

All china is "ceramic," which means it is made of clay and baked, but there are wide differences which you will readily recognize when shopping.

Fine china is made of fine clays and fired to achieve nonporosity. Though it appears fragile, it has great durability and translucency.

American china is justly famous for its ivory body, produced through a special hardening agent. English bone china contains a mixture of bone ash added to the procelain, which gives it its characteristic whiteness, great strength and translucency.

Some of the quality names among the china and porcelain ware include the English Spode, Wedgwood, Staffordshire, Royal Worcester and Crown Derby; from Germany, Dresden and Rosenthal; Limoges and Sèvres from France; American Lenox (since 1889) and many other American names which stand for the same beauty and quality that is found in the imports.

Earthenware lends itself well to modern shapes and designs, and in its finer forms closely resembles china. It generally costs less, and is less formal in appearance, though there are some designs which are as expensive as plain china. It is opaque, porous and fully glazed, but softer and less durable than the wares made of more refined clay and fired at higher temperatures. Because of the soft-textured body, it offers little resistance to cracking and chipping, but is stronger than pottery. It boasts some lovely gay patterns and reproductions of favored Old World porcelains, and it is usually available both in place settings and in sixteen-piece starter sets.

Pottery, the bulkiest and heaviest of the three principal dinnerwares, is, like earthenware, opaque and porous. It lends itself to free-hand designs applied in bright primitive colors. Often uneven in texture and shape, it is effective for decorative pieces, either in glazed or unglazed finish. Pottery for everyday use is chosen for its durability and casual look, and is popular in its many designs of oven-to-table ware.

To test the difference between earthenware and china, hold a piece of china to the light. You will recognize its translucent qualities when you see your fingers silhouetted through it. Also, try striking it with a pencil or your fingernail, and listen to its bell-like tone.

Tap a piece of earthenware with a pencil, and you'll hear a dull, heavy sound. And as a further test, if you ever have the opportunity of testing a broken piece of fine china, you'll find that though the glaze may be chipped, it will not absorb even a drop of water or grease. Earthenware, however, is so porous, it acts as blotting paper.

The quality and price of china depends on its styling, thinness, type of glaze and decoration. The two types of decoration used on china and earthenware are underglaze and overglaze.

In the underglaze process the decoration is put on the body before the glaze is baked, making it durable and permanent. It will withstand unlimited use without changing color or texture, and will not wash off even in the hottest water.

Overglaze decorations are applied to the surface of the finishing glaze. The ware is then placed in the kiln or oven and the colors are fused with the glaze at a moderate temperature. This process of surface finishing is quite popular because it offers a wider range of colors.

There are two kinds of gold decoration: coin gold and luster gold. Coin gold is pure gold which is burnished or rubbed to a soft sheen. Luster gold gives a bright golden surface but contains only a small amount of pure gold, and is considerably lower in price.

Etched-gold designs are sometimes called "encrusted gold." They are seen on costly dinnerware, unusual service plates and decorative pieces. The design is etched in the glaze with acid, and coin gold is applied to the etched portion. After burnishing, the etched design stands out against the duller background.

Molded Plastic Dinnerware

This type of dinnerware is very popular for casual use because of its practical qualities. Virtually unbreakable, it can be placed in a dishwasher without harm, and it is resistant to chipping and cracking. It is not resistant to an open flame or oven heat, however.

Traditional designs and attractive colors are available in wide variety.

Check plastic dinnerware for uniformity in texture, color and molding. Look for smooth edges and pieces that are easy to handle. This dinnerware is usually sold in sets, and available in open stock.

Deciding Factors

1. Be sure that the china pattern you select reflects you and your best taste, and is suitable to the life you'll lead.

2. Before you decide, actually set a table with it, trying different cloths, silver and glassware. Then ask yourself some questions: Does it thrill you just to look at it? Will it be a versatile pattern? Artistic? Mix well with other china? Above all, is it plain enough to be pleasing over a long period of time?

3. Does the bridegroom-to-be share your enthusiasm for it?

4. Buy the best quality you can possibly afford. Cheap dinnerware is a poor investment because it chips readily, and soon you'll have only odds and ends.

5. Don't just "look" at the china when you are making a selection. Examine the various pieces to check the feel of them. Lift the cup to see if it handles well. Is the handle easily grasped, and large enough for a man's fingers? Do the teapots and pitchers pour well and clean easily? Guard against spindly legs on any piece of china, as they break easily.

6. Check patterns in the daylight as well as in artificial light. See that base colors are even, not mottled or streaked.

Another characteristic of fine china is its perfect balance. Make sure that the pieces stand firmly and evenly by examining a few carefully for all these minute details.

Minimum Requirements for China

Your "budget" list for fine dinnerware would be service for four, with a few extra cups and saucers, and dessert plates. The dessert plates will be more interesting if chosen in a harmonizing pattern, for variety.

This amount of china will serve you only temporarily, however, so it is best to aim for at least eight place settings:

  8 dinner plates (10 inches in diameter)
  8 bread and butter plates (6 inches in diameter)
12 salad or dessert plates, may also be used for place plates (8 inches in diameter)
  8 cups and saucers
  8 soup plates (or cream soups and saucers)
  1 teapot (china or silver)
  1 cream and sugar (china or silver)
  2 vegetable dishes

1 large platter (china or silver)
1 smaller platter (china or silver)

In addition to the pieces listed, you may wish to have demitasse cups and saucers for after-dinner coffee. Extra pieces, such as bowls, sauceboat and stand for gravies, salad bowl, condiment dishes, salt and pepper sets, bread tray or wicker basket and individual table ash trays are also necessary items to complete a table setting.

This list is necessarily flexible. You will want to make changes according to your needs and your manner of living. And again, a reminder that fine china is not fragile, to be put on a high shelf and used only on special occasions. It should be used often and enjoyed.

Your more informal tableware should include a charming set of breakfast dishes, with service for six, at least. Cereal bowls, egg cups, syrup jug, a covered toast dish, platters and serving bowls are all necessary for everyday living; also salt and pepper sets, wooden salad bowls, and serving dishes that go from stove to table.

Into the informal class usually fall the many exciting dishes for buffet dining. Here you are completely on your own. There are many gaily decorated pottery pieces and copper, pewter or brass accessories that will make your table gleam.

SELECTING YOUR SILVER

Your silver will be one of your most prized possessions and should be chosen with great and loving care. Since you'll be treasuring it "as long as you both shall live," it is important that your husband-to-be approves of the pattern. Why not go shopping together? Evaluate the patterns, studying each in relation to your other tableware and your general taste in living. The decision should rightly be made by the two of you, with no outside influences.

While shopping, check the feel and balance of each piece of silver in your own hand, just as though you were actually using it at the table. Test the smoothness of the fork tines and the strength of the shanks. Try handling the knife. Is it comfortable? Before making your selection-for-a-lifetime, try a setting of your silver with your chosen china and any other table accoutrements already in your possession. Have a dress rehearsal with different types and colors of tablecloths and analyze the over-all effects.

Sterling silver is the best silver you can buy, and is required by law to contain 92.5 per cent silver. Copper is added to harden and increase its wearing qualities. The official stamp of "sterling" placed on the back of each piece of silver indicates its purity and is known as a hallmark.

There are two finishes in sterling, or solid, silver. They are (1) a bright shiny polished surface, or (2) a duller finish called the butler finish.

Oxidation is a darkening process applied to ornate designs of sterling flatware. It increases their beauty by giving rich contrasts. Designs are made by these three methods:

(1) chased, or engraved by hand
(2) embossed, by impressing with a mold
(3) etched by the use of acid

Patina is the soft tracery of minute scratches which silver attains as it is used and properly cared for. It is this soft, mellow finish which lends great charm to silver, and is often seen in heirloom pieces.

What Type of Pattern for You?

Do you favor richly ornamented period designs? Or are you naturally drawn to the more contemporary patterns?

It isn't necessary that your silver be matched to the exact period of your other furnishings. Your main consideration should be to choose a pattern of good basic design that will harmonize well with your table appointments and compliment your way of life.

There are two main classifications from which to

choose: modern and traditional. The contemporary or modern designs are characterized by their simplicity and daintiness of motif. Many have delicate flower or leaf decorations. Others are severely plain, depending upon shape for their smartness and style. Traditional silver patterns reflect the decorative tone of a particular historical era. As a rule, a simple design in silver is more desirable because it adapts to a greater assortment of ornate designs in companion pieces on the table. When ornate silver is selected, it is well to co-ordinate it with simple designs in china and glassware. It is an erroneous idea that ornate silver is more difficult to clean, since modern up-to-date polishes make all silver fairly easy to keep shining.

Sterling flatware is usually sold by the place setting, though it is always available by the piece. A basic place setting consists of six pieces: a knife, fork, salad (or dessert) fork, teaspoon, butter spreader and place spoon for soup, cereal or dessert.

Though sterling is expensive, it is a sound investment and one that will gather tradition from generation to generation. Sterling patterns are rarely discontinued, and sets may be added to as the years progress.

Is the pattern you are considering a medium-weight or heavy-weight design? The heavy weight contains more sterling and naturally is more expensive. Usually the very ornate patterns are in this class. When silver is described as being of medium or average weight (as the majority of patterns are today), it does not necessarily mean that the wearing quality of the silver will be affected. Medium-weight sterling is still heavy enough to withstand generations of wear.

The amount of handwork which has been given to each silver piece is also a determining factor on the price. The die method is used to stamp the design on each separate piece. If the finishing touches require intricate handwork, the cost of such skilled labor adds to the price of the product. Hand-wrought silver, which is fashioned almost entirely by hand, is the most expensive of all silver and in a class of luxury all its own.

Study the designs of the patterns you are considering from the standpoint of good proportion and good contour. Even an untrained eye can sense the lack of symmetry and harmony in pieces of silver if the design is not good. Good balance is another point to check. You'll find that in well-designed forks, spoons and knives, good balance is immediately recognized by the even distribution of weight when the pieces are held in the hand.

You can depend on a reliable dealer to advise you unbiasedly on your silver. And you can also rely on the trademarks of the old established silversmiths. Look on the back of each piece for the sterling mark stamp and the maker's name for added assurance of quality and excellence of design.

How Much to Buy

The amount of silver you will want to aim for certainly should be no less than service for eight. This may not be attainable right in the beginning of your marriage, but if you let your desires be known (what with anniversaries and holiday gifts coming your way), it won't take very long to complete this basic number of place settings.

You should take under advisement the question of whether to get luncheon knives and forks, or the larger and more expensive dinner sizes. Many brides find the luncheon size adequate for all the entertaining they wish to do. If you plan to entertain formally, however, you should include the dinner sizes on your list, for at formal affairs only the dinner-size fork and knife should be used for the main course.

Also, when making up your place settings, if you prefer, you may substitute *two* teaspoons in place of the cream-soup spoon and the *one* teaspoon.

As a guide to build toward, here is a basic list of flat silver:

8 knives	4 tablespoons
8 forks	1 cold meat fork
16 teaspoons	1 two-piece steak set
8 salad forks	1 sugar spoon or tongs
8 butter spreaders	1 gravy ladle
8 cream-soup spoons	1 butter knife
8 dessert spoons	1 cake knife

The ideal set includes both sizes of knives and forks, making sixteen available for serving a large buffet. Also, if you serve seafood you'll want oyster or cocktail forks. If you serve demitasse, you'll need the small coffee spoons. These may be in a different pattern.

Silver Plate

If it seems to be out of the question to have even a starter set of sterling, don't despair, but go shopping for a pretty pattern of silver plate in a fine quality ware, and you'll find it will serve you well for many years to come.

It wasn't until a little over a century ago that any but the most wealthy families could afford silver on the table because of its excessive cost. Then the electroplating process was invented, in which a base metal is coated or plated with pure silver. The best grade of silver plating is made from refined nickel silver with a heavy deposit of pure silver. The thickness of the silver varies with the manufacturers and depends mainly on the length of time the piece is submerged and how often. Better qualities of silver plate have reinforcement at the points of greatest wear. This is very important to the life of your flatware, so insist on this feature as a guarantee for better service. The reinforcing may be done by an inlaid process, where an extra block of silver is inlaid at the wear points (such as at the backs of spoons) or by an overlaid process, which means wear points are given an extra coating of silver on top of the plating. You should look for good balance and fine design in your silver pattern, and check the pieces for smooth edges and an even silver coating.

You can buy silver plate in sets, with service for six, eight or twelve. Or it may be purchased by the place setting, if you prefer, just as sterling silver is. The fifty-two piece service for eight is a favorite for brides. It customarily comes in a tarnish-proof case, as do all the complete services. Most of the patterns are open stock, so that you can add to them when you wish.

Sheffield silver is silver-coated sheet copper, a form of fine silver-plating which was in use in England before the electroplating process was invented. A sheet of pure silver was fused by heat to each side of a sheet of copper, and the metal was handled almost like sterling silver. The famed gadroon edge, which is typical of Sheffield, was formed from silver added to conceal the copper at the edges. Most pieces of genuine Sheffield plate to be found today are highly prized for their exceptional beauty.

Other Flatware

Metals other than sterling silver and silver plate are available today in handsome flatware. They include several types of gold metals featured both in flatware service and holloware, which are a combination of alloys plated over a silver base. The designs usually are perfectly plain, with the emphasis on smartness and simplicity of line in each individual piece. In some of these wares the knives can be sharpened and the flatware, polished like silver. Other types require no polishing and are guaranteed to withstand washing in an electric dishwasher. These glowing gold metals set a dramatic table and are available by the piece or in place settings. Most of them (with the exception of solid gold-plate) are less expensive than sterling.

Stainless steel flatware is very popular among the young marrieds because of its appealing modern designs, its durability and resistance to stains. Many well-styled patterns—both American and imported—are offered today, and may be used handsomely with informal dinnerware, for buffet or patio entertaining as well as every day use. Stainless steel comes in a satin finish and a mirror effect. Avoid the finish that is "tinny" looking. Examine each piece as you would silver. Check rims of spoon bowls, tips of fork tines and the in-between spaces for smoothness and evenness. In general, flatware with hollow handles is more expensive.

Suggested List for Holloware

Holloware (the platters, bowls, etc., used in table service) are made in both sterling and in silver-plated ware. The former, of course, is the more expensive. It isn't at all necessary that the silver pieces match, but it adds a note of smartness to your table if they do complement each other.

Much to the delight of brides, holloware is one of the most favored wedding-gift selections. In order that you may muse over the luxuries which you would like to own, here is a list to guide you in the choices you may want to register with the wedding-gift counselor in your favorite store.

silver tea service
after-dinner coffee
    service
large platter
steak platter with well-
    and-tree design
double vegetable dish
    with cover
gravy boat and tray
candlesticks (tall
    and short)

water pitcher
sauce bowl and tray
pipkin and tray
salt-and-pepper shakers
ash trays
bread tray
bowls—small, medium
    and large
sandwich tray for
    canapés, cake, etc.

Monograms

Whether or not silver should be monogrammed is a matter of personal choice. If you decide on monogramming, you may have one initial, or three. If one is to be used, it should be either that of your maiden name or the first letter of your husband's last name. In a three-letter monogram, the first initials of the bride and groom may be combined with the first letter of their last name, and usually the initial of the last name is larger than the ones on each side of it. For instance, if you are Jane and Mark Phillips, the initials could be in the formation: J P M. Or, the initials arranged in a triangle form, with the last-name initial at the top of the triangle and the first initials of each of your given names placed at the bottom. Or the monogram may be made up of the bride's three initials, given name, her maiden surname and her married surname, JBP for Jane Barker Phillips.

Let your silverware pattern be your guide when selecting the style of lettering. There are elongated block monograms, inverted triangles, script-type letters that intertwine, and many other interesting shapes from which to choose. Simple letters look best on simple patterns, delicate letters on the most ornate designs. Old English letters lend themselves appropriately to the use of a single surname initial.

The usual custom is to place the monogram on the front of each piece. But if the design is quite patterned and you still desire a monogram, you may have it placed on the back, following the French custom. Monogram letters may be embossed (raised), or engraved (sunken).

Silver trays, tea or coffee services, and other hollo-ware pieces are often engraved with large monograms, or highly stylized initials, worked out in individual designs.

CHOOSING YOUR GLASSWARE

Your glassware will add much sparkle and beauty to your table setting and should be chosen directly to complement your china and silver. The only way to really be sure of this is to have a dress rehearsal of the complete place settings, seeing all three components together, right in the shop where you are making selections. (This can usually be arranged where special services for brides are the order of the day.)

Since glassware is always such a favored gift, it is advisable to register the pattern of your choice early enough to be of benefit to your shower-giving friends. And chances are you will want to wait until after the wedding to purchase any glassware yourself.

Your first selection will probably be stemware to go with your fine china, and most likely you'll want to select crystal for its clear sparkling beauty and look of elegance. It differs from ordinary glass because of its special lead content, which adds a clear brilliance and metallic sheen.

In order to appreciate to the utmost your new glassware, you may like to know something about the art of making glass. From a technical standpoint, glass is composed mostly of silica sand, soda ash and potash lead or lime. These components are fused together at a very high temperature and cooled under carefully controlled conditions. There are two methods of shaping molten glass, one by blowing and the other by pressing.

Blown glass is the lightest, thinnest, clearest of glass, and includes the finest quality stemware, such as goblets, cocktail glasses, wine glasses, etc. These hand-blown pieces depend greatly on the skill and artistry of the blower, as the making of this type of glass is almost entirely a human operation, and consequently the most expensive.

There are three kinds of blown glass. All will sing out with a singing bell tone when gently tapped with a pencil.

1. *Off-hand blown glass* is completely hand-wrought and is the finest and most costly type of glass made. It is mouth-blown by highly skilled experts and formed without the aid of molds. The artistry of this process continues right on through the finishing and polishing of the glass, which is done by hand.

2. *Hand-blown glass* is a combination of the mouth-blowing process with molding and hand-fabricating. Though clever craftsmanship is required in this process because of the machine work involved, the cost of production is somewhat less.

3. *Machine-blown glass* is the least expensive of all blown glass, since the liquid glass is put into molds by an automatic feeder and shaped by compressed air.

Pressed glass is formed by pouring the molten liquid into molds. It is cooled and then reheated by a "finisher" with a paddle, who spins the piece to the finished shape. The glass is tempered and put through special polishing and inspection processes before its completion. This process is used to make heavier stemware of all sorts; also weightier pieces such as vases, bowls, plates and sculptured forms. Pressed glass has strength and toughness. It will not ring clearly when tapped, but this fact does not lessen its value.

Decoration of Glassware

Glassware is decorated in many ways. There is etched glass, cut glass and engraved glass. Gold or platinum decorations may be brushed or stamped on, then fired into the glass. Enameled motifs are usually applied by a screen process and baked on for permanency. On cheaper glassware the designs are often merely painted on and allowed to dry without baking, so that they often wear off.

Sand carving is one of the most modern decorative devices. The design is sand-blasted on the surface of the glass through a mask. This results in a gray satin-finish decoration.

How to Judge Good Glass

1. Good glassware should have clarity and luster. Quality glassware is sparkling clear with a permanent polish. Colored glass should reflect true tones and consistency in its shadings.

2. Smoothness and regularity are important. Check for beady or scratchy edges indicative of inferior workmanship.

3. Look for well-balanced symmetrical shapes. There should be a pleasing balance between the bowl and stem of goblets.

4. Study the decoration. If etched, even the most delicate detail should be distinct, with no acid spots or breaks in lines. Clear brilliance is an indication of superior etching. If it is a cut-glass decoration, the cuttings should be sharp and true. Ornamentation should not appear out of proportion or merely "slapped on." (Be especially alert to this when working out a monogram for glassware.)

5. Examine carefully for defects in glass. Quality glass should be free from waves, specks or bubbles. Avoid unusually prominent mold marks and discernible seams on pressed glass.

6. When shopping for colored glass, check every piece you are considering in artificial light as well as daylight. Blues, and many other colors too, change tone in different lightings.

7. The trademark of the manufacturer is the best assurance of all when his reliability is unquestionable. Buy from well-established stores and choose open-stock patterns so that you will know that the merchandise will continue to be sold over a period of time.

How Much to Buy

Glassware is sold by the place setting, just as with china and silver. The most favored setting consists of a water goblet, sherbet or champagne, and a medium wine glass. The sherbet may be used for champagne, sherbet, fruit or any suitable dessert. It could be used for a fish cocktail. The medium wine glass may double for fruit juices and cocktails. If you prefer, your place settings could include iced-tea glasses, juice glasses and salad plates, along with goblets and the sherbets.

Storage space more than anything else will no doubt be the determining factor in the amount of glassware you list.

Here are the average glassware requirements:

Glassware for the Table

8 water goblets	8 sherbets
8 juice glasses	8 salad plates

Optional

8 stemmed wine glasses	8 stemmed champagne
8 stemmed sherry	glasses
glasses	8 liqueur glasses

Bar accessories, if you are interested in having them, should come under your husband's jurisdiction. So why not take him shopping with you and let him take the lead in your selections? There's endless variety in glassware of this type. The number of glasses you'll need for the bar depends entirely on how many you will be entertaining at one time, how often you entertain and your selections in drinks. The average-size beverage glasses (highball size) hold fourteen to sixteen ounces, and may be used for iced tea, lemonade or any tall drink. Old-fashioned cocktail glasses are standard size, and make nice fruit or tomato juice glasses also.

If the glasses you choose are plain, you may want to have them smartly monogrammed.

Other Selections in Glass

There's beautiful glass available in all shapes and for practically every purpose. You'll want to include on your gift-preference lists several sizes and shapes of vases and bowls for flowers. What about pitchers, ash trays and a lovely cigarette box, perhaps?

Decorative bottles in colored glass are effective to

liven a corner. Figurines of fine glass, candy jars, crystal candelabra or low candlesticks—all are usable and exciting pieces to own and treasure for years to come.

CHAPTER 10 | To Have and To Hold

It's an altogether exciting world when those white-tissued, beribboned packages start coming in. We warn you, though, that chaos undoubtedly will set in unless you get a firm grip on your pen and a gift-record book and get organized beforehand.

1. Check to see that you have an adequate supply of thank-you notepaper and stamps. It's better to have an oversupply than to run short at the last hectic moment. Arrange a special place for them and see that they are kept in their place when not in use.

2. Get a gift-record book with numbered stickers. (These may be purchased at any stationery department.) As each gift arrives, enter the number of the gift, the name of the donor, date and description on the gift list pages. Be accurate about this and it will save you many a headache.

3. Acknowledge each gift the day it arrives if at all possible. Set aside a certain hour each day to do this.

4. Arrange a suitable place for your gifts. (It is quite proper to display them at your wedding reception if you have room.)

DISPLAYING YOUR GIFTS

Remove all the large pieces of furniture from the room which you have chosen for the display of your gifts.

If card tables aren't adequate, why not trestle tables? They can be rented, or possibly borrowed from the church, and arranged around the side of the room and down the center.

Most etiquette books say to cover the tables with plain white damask cloths, but with all the exciting materials on the market, it seems a little tame to use plain white linen. (And who has that many matching banquet cloths, anyway?) Several yards of inexpensive material in soft peach or powder-blue to blend with the color scheme of the room would be much more artistic. You can use the material later for another purpose. There are sheer fabrics, glazed ones, metallics, plain materials and shimmering ones.

Your shower gifts may be arranged all together on one table or mixed in with other gifts.

Most people of discernment agree that donors' cards should be removed from the gifts when they are displayed. It is actually a matter which you and your family may decide, however, for there is no reason as far as propriety goes why cards shouldn't be left with the gifts. Everyone will want to know who gave you this and that, so someone in the family should be responsible for giving out this information.

Don't display your checks (if you are lucky enough to receive some), but you may mention them and their donors. "Uncle Arthur sent us a check for our bedroom furniture," or whatever.

Be sure to take out a temporary floater insurance policy for your gifts while they are on display. During the reception you may want to have on hand a plainclothes man to guard the gifts if there are many costly ones.

WRITING YOUR THANK-YOU NOTES

This is the part you dread, isn't it? Well, it may tax the gray matter a bit to dash off a dozen or so notes a day, but after all it's an important aspect of wedding etiquette and good manners.

Don't hold back your enthusiasm because you think it sounds school-girlish. Most people love exuberance, especially when it's over something they selected for you.

Don't forget to write thank-you notes for your shower gifts and a note of appreciation to your party hostesses. Since many of your closest friends will probably give you more than one shower gift, wait until near your wedding date (after all the parties are over) and write thank-you notes to include all the shower presents each has given you. In this instance you don't need to mention them by name, if there is quite a list, but write a general "thank-you" for everything.

Although the wedding gifts belong to you, the bride, try to include the bridegroom in your letter of thanks.

When wedding gifts are sent by a married couple, direct your note to the wife. You may mention her husband, if you choose, but usually "you" is understood to mean "you both."

Refer to the gift specifically when you write the donors. If you are in a quandary as to what it is, speak of it as "your silver piece" (or china, glass, or whatever it is).

Here are a few ideas to get started:

Dear Mrs. Warner:
Your handsome Venetian glass ash tray is now on our coffee table and in constant use. Jim loves it for its big size, and we both send many, many thanks for this treasured addition to our new household.

Jim has spoken so glowingly of you and Mr. Warner and I'm looking forward to the opportunity of meeting you when you come East the very next time.

In the meantime, our sincere regards to Mr. Warner, and bless you both for your sweet thoughtfulness in remembering us at this happy time.

> Most sincerely,
> Jean Barton

Dear Mrs. Cushing:

What dears you were to select such a lovely lamp for our new home. It not only fits into our blue and white color scheme beautifully, but it pleases the practical housewife side of my nature because of its washable shade. I'll try always to keep it as gleaming white as it is now.

Jim joins me in hoping that you will be among the first to come see us when we return the middle of October.

> Affectionately,
> Jean Barton

Dear Miss Edith:

To think that you should have taken time out of your busy life to make this marvelous needlepoint for me! I can't tell you how very much both Jim and I appreciate your sweet thoughtfulness—and thank you!

We're looking forward to seeing you on our wedding day.

> Most sincerely,
> Jean

Marilyn—you dear:

Now you will *have* to come up soon and see our etchings and us.

How did you know that Jim and I both were yearning for those particular contemporary ones for either side of the living-room windows? Nothing could have pleased us more, and we love you for it.

Do come to tea next Wednesday afternoon and see our gifts.

> Till then,
> Jean

Dear Mrs. Carewe:

Ever since I was a little girl I have adored quaint little objects of art. Now, to have that precious white circus horse with its brilliant trappings for my very own in our new home is really a thrill.

Jim thinks it is one of the cleverest decorative pieces he has ever seen—so, you see, we are both proud owners.

Bring Mr. Carewe and come visit us, and the new pet, at our apartment very soon.

Most sincerely,
Jean Barton

WHEN A GIFT HAS TO BE RETURNED

Dear Mrs. James:

You were so kind to send us those lovely demitasse spoons and we do appreciate your thought of us. I want to tell you, though, what happened, and I hope you'll approve.

We discovered that we had two dozen demitasse spoons and only six demitasse cups and saucers. So we took the liberty of exchanging your gift for another half-dozen matching cups and saucers in our china pattern. Now our service for after-dinner coffee is complete, and we are delighted.

Jim and I send our sincere thanks to you and Mr. James and hope that you will come soon to see us.

Most sincerely,
Jean Barton Smith

Unless you know that someone has spent a great deal of time and effort in selecting a certain wedding gift, it is perfectly correct to exchange a present if you feel so inclined. Gift donors expect you to take back a gift if it is duplicated. Let your good taste be your guide, however, and don't do a mass exchange.

When a wedding is definitely called off, all gifts must be returned by the bride's family. If the wedding is merely postponed an announcement is sent to guests and the presents are not returned (*See* page 88).

SPECIAL QUESTIONS AND ANSWERS

Q. Are printed "thank-you" cards ever permissible?

A. Printed "thank-yous" are never permissible, but often in a large wedding where there is a great rush of gifts, engraved cards acknowledging the receipt of the present may be sent out with the promise of a personal note to follow. This is one way of reassuring gift senders that their presents arrived safely, if it is impossible to make acknowledgement immediately. Stationers and jewelers carry samples of these forms, but it is not advisable to resort to this method unless unavoidable.

It goes without saying that you should follow up with personal thank-you notes as soon as possible.

Q. How should acknowledgment be made when a wedding gift is sent from a large group of fellow employees in an office?

A. When individual names are listed on the gift card a personal note should be written to each contributor. An all-inclusive note may be sent to the office, addressed to the leader of the group, if a general "From Your Office" card is the only one enclosed with gift. If the gift is in the form of a check or a gift certificate, it is well to make mention in your thank-you note of what you intend to buy for your home as a lasting remembrance from this group of friends.

FOR YOUR ATTENDANTS

Although you are on the receiving end for most of the gifts during your pre-nuptial days, there are a few tokens of appreciation which you yourself will want to give. Bridesmaids' gifts, customarily, are all alike. The maid or matron of honor may receive a more personalized present of slightly greater value. Gifts such as a bracelet or brooch, lockets, gold heart pendants, perfume atomizers or evening bags are all appropriate. The larger and more elaborate the wedding, the more valuable the gifts, though no bride should give such lavish gifts that they set a precedent difficult for future brides in the group to follow.

Short single-strand pearls, a pair of silver barrettes or a dainty bracelet all make appropriate gifts for little flower girls.

FROM THE BRIDEGROOM TO HIS ATTENDANTS

The ushers' gifts should all be alike and may take the form of gold belt buckles, gold-mounted fountain pens, cuff links, cigarette cases or sterling silver money clips.

The best man usually rates a special gift. It may well be a piece of luggage, a case of rare liquor, a lined leather billfold or even a wrist watch.

At a formal daytime wedding the bridegroom may give his ushers their vests, ties and gloves to make for uniformity.

When to Present the Attendants' Gifts

Each gift should be appropriately boxed and wrapped with special wedding paper, ready to present to attendants at the bridesmaids' luncheon and the bachelor dinner respectively. They may be given at the bridal dinner the night before the wedding if there are no separate bride and bridegroom parties.

GIFTS TO OTHER FRIENDS WHO SERVE AT YOUR WEDDING

Friends who are engaged to play or sing at your wedding or reception may refuse to accept a fee. In such cases gifts from you would be in order. They also should be presented at the bridal dinner.

It's a gracious gesture to send a corsage to any woman who is taking part in your wedding, but this courtesy does not take the place of a more lasting personal gift.

Young girls who may have been asked to assist in the dining room at the reception should receive some sort of small remembrance in behalf of their services.

FROM THE BRIDE TO THE GROOM

There's nothing obligatory about the gift-giving custom between bride and groom, but it's usual in the large formal wedding.

What you choose to give each other is a personal matter, but gifts should have a sentimental keepsake quality. (Not articles of clothing, however.)

Often the bridegroom presents his bride with an heirloom brooch, lovely matched pearls, a bracelet or jeweled watch. You, in turn, may give him a dated and monogrammed watch, gold cuff links, matched luggage, a handsome wallet with his name plate, a movie camera, or even a fine chess set. You'll know what he wants!

CHAPTER 11 | **Strains of Lohengrin**

When the organ begins its whispered note, you'll probably be too excited to know what it's playing. But all the others will be there to enjoy and appreciate the music in full measure of its enchantment, so choose the musical selections for your wedding with great care.

PRELIMINARY MUSIC

The incidental music, which will begin about a half hour before the ceremony, should be of classical type. Selections from any of the old masters, such as Mendelssohn, Wagner, Brahms and Schubert, are always appropriate to such an occasion.

Following is a program of incidental music for a formal church wedding as suggested in *The Cokesbury Marriage Manual*. It's your privilege as a bride, however, to consult with your organist and make your selections together.

"Allegro" and "Pastorale" from
    First Symphony .... *Guilmant*

"Fugue" from Toccata and
    Fugue in C .... *Bach*
"Prelude in G Major" .... *Bach*
"Festival March" .... *A. Foote*
"Grand Triumphal Chorus" ..... *Guilmant*
"Ave Maria Lourdes"
    Traditional music arranged by *Pietro Yon*
"Adagio in A Minor" .... *Bach*
"Panis Angelicus" .... *Franck*
"Choral in G Minor" .... *Bach*
"March Pontificale" ...... *De la Tombelle*

Are You Having a Vocalist?

If you plan to have vocal music by a church choir, a quartet or a soloist, remember that many churches permit only their own choir or soloists to sing in the church. Also, many churches have a ruling that all wedding music, vocal and instrumental, must be approved by their choir directors. You'd better be sure to check this with your organist before you make your final selections.

Don't schedule more than two vocal selections. This musical program should take place after most of the guests have arrived and are seated. You might time the last song to take place just before the wedding march, while the mothers are being escorted to their places.

Be sure to have the vocalist go through his or her part of the program at your rehearsal so that it may be clocked to the minute.

Here are a few vocal selections as suggestions:

"I Follow Thee Also" ....*J. S. Bach*
    (from the St. John Passion)
"My Heart Ever Faithful" ......*J. S. Bach*
    (from the Pentecost Cantata)
"Be Thou Contented" ....*J. S. Bach*
"Entreat Me Not to Leave
    Thee" ....*C. F. Gounod*

Note: It will be a welcome innovation if you and the bridegroom have a significant poem that can be sung to special music, or an appropriate hymn that you both treasure.

Though such musical numbers as "I Love You Truly," "Liebestraum," "Oh Promise Me" and "Meditation from Thais" have become associated with weddings in the minds of many, these selections are not sacred enough for most church standards, and should not be considered as wedding music. If you have a special attachment for any of these, you may put them on the list for the musicians to play at the reception.

The chants of the *Messa pro Sponsa et Sponsa* are available for solo and choral use as incidental nuptial music:

> *Introit:* The God of Israel (*Deus Israel*), from Tobit 7-8
>
> *Gradual:* Thy wife (*Uxor tua*), from Psalm 128
>
> *Verse:* The Lord Send thee Help, from Psalm 20 (mode viii)
>
> *Verse:* The Lord that made Heaven, from Psalm 134 (mode iv)
>
> *Tract:* Behold, that thus, from Psalm 128 (mode viii)
>
> *Offertory:* I trusted in thee, from Psalm 31 (mode ii)

One or more stanzas of the following hymns make excellent solos or choir numbers. In some cases the tunes will serve admirably as simple processional and recessional music.

> "O perfect love," Barnby
> "The voice that breathed o'er Eden" (tune: St. Alphege, Gauntlett)
> "O Father, all creating" (tune: Ellacombe)
> "O blest the house" (tune: Retreat, Hastings)

"Let me be thine forever" (tune: *Ich dank dir, lieber Herre*)

"Jesus, thou joy of loving hearts" (tune: *Christe Redemptor*, mode i)

Preliminary Music for Home Wedding

If you are having an electric organ, a string organ, a string trio (two violins and a cello) or a harp and trio (two violins and a cello) or a harp and violin, the preliminary music might include such selections as:

"Spring Song" . . . . *Mendelssohn*
"Toujours L'Amour" . . . . *Friml*
"Dreams" . . . . *Schumann*
"Aria of Nicolanta" from *Lakme,* played by cello
"Song of Songs" . . . . *Rimsky-Korsakov*
(for voice)
March . . . .*Svendsen*

Give your instructions in writing to the organist or musicians who are to play at your wedding. It will help prevent any misunderstandings.

MUSIC FOR THE PROCESSIONAL AND RECESSIONAL

The "Bridal Chorus" from the third act of *Lohengrin* usually is chosen for the processional, followed by Mendelssohn's "Wedding March" for the recessional. These selections are not at all compulsory, however, if you prefer some variations. But it *is* important that the music you select has a satisfactory rhythm and timing for walking down the aisle. The organist will serve as your guide and will set the pace for the wedding party at your rehearsal.

DURING THE CEREMONY

If you wish to have soft music played during the ceremony, you might consider a beloved hymn or an appropriate religious favorite from Dvorák's Biblical Songs. The selection should be meaningful to the two of you.

Often, at the very close of the ceremony, organ chimes are played or the ringing of the carillon bells is heard just before the organist breaks into Mendelssohn's "Wedding March."

Or you might want to have "The Lord's Prayer" sung very softly by a single voice or small chorus.

RECEPTION MUSIC

Your party music should be light and gay, and could include all your special preferences in semiclassical music, show tunes, folk tunes and old-time favorites. You may have a string trio, an electric organ, an accordion or—a small orchestra to play for dancing. The music should start the minute the bride and groom arrive at the reception, and continue softly during the receiving period. The orchestra customarily breaks into a stepped-up version of "Here Comes the Bride" as soon as the bridal pair leaves the receiving line.

The musicians should be given a list of the selections you want played.

CHAPTER 12 | **Memories to Cherish**

Your wedding reception is *really* a party, and should be a heavenly affair, whether it's under the old peach tree or atop a skyscraper hotel.

Your home is the logical place to entertain. It's practical because your gifts will be there on display, your going-away clothes will be waiting in your own room for you to step into them . . . and sentimentally speaking, it's home, sweet home.

If your home is too small for a large reception, how about your aunt's big house or the home of your mother's best friend? There is always someone who would be overjoyed to fill her house with flowers and play hostess to such a joyous gathering . . . with your family paying the bills, of course. A town or country club or a hotel ballroom offer the next best solutions, though they lack the personal background and may add to your expenses.

For a small wedding you might invite your friends to your new apartment after the ceremony, to drink a toast and wish you happiness.

THE RECEIVING LINE

The receiving line is usually formed just inside the entrance to the room where the reception is being held, with guests moving from left to right. Your mother, as the hostess, should be first in line, with the bridegroom's father next, then the bridegroom's mother, the bride's father, the bride, groom, maid of honor and brides-maids all in a row. This arrangement gives your mother an opportunity to present the parents of the bridegroom to all the guests. However, it is optional whether or not your father stands in line. He may move about, greeting the guests on his own as the host of the party. When he is not in the line, the bridegroom's mother stands next to the bride's mother.

If it is a very formal affair, it is customary to have the bride's father in the receiving line, particularly if the groom's parents are not known in the community. In some cases, when the groom's father is well acquainted with most of the guests, it is permissible to have only the two mothers stand in line with the bride, groom and the bridal attendants. In this kind of setup, the fathers should remain in the neighborhood of the receiving line, to see that introductions are made and that guests are directed to the refreshment tables.

Another acceptable variation of the receiving line includes having two separate groups. In such an arrangement, the parents of both the bride and the bridegroom receive just inside the door, with the bride and groom and the others forming a line at a conveniently located spot further into the room, or on the opposite side.

The ushers and best man have no place in the receiving line, but make themselves as useful as possible. Often the head usher (or any selected usher) acts as announcer, asking the names of the guests as they appear in the receiving line and presenting each, in turn, to the bride's mother. She always introduces the guests to the groom's parents, who pass the name down the line to the bride and groom.

You, the bride, still in full wedding costume, may continue to hold your bouquet in your left hand as you stand in the receiving line. Or you may place it carefully aside, to be picked up just before making the grand entrance into the dining room, on the arm of the bridegroom. Your attendants will hold their bouquets (in their left hands) throughout the receiving period, since their flowers are a co-ordinate part of their costumes.

If long gloves are part of your formal costume, you need not remove them until refreshments are about to be served. (The same rule follows for all feminine members of the wedding party.) The mothers, if wearing hats, will leave them on throughout the reception.

All men of the wedding party will remove their gloves and leave them with their coats upon arrival at the reception.

As the bride, you will present the bridegroom to anyone he does not know. He will likewise introduce his relatives or friends to you, unless the guest is a much older woman, in which case he will present you to her.

Conversations should be fairly brief if the line is long. You'll have time later to talk it all over with your closest friends.

PLANNING THE DETAILS OF THE RECEPTION

If your wedding reception is to be a big affair, you will certainly want to turn over all responsibility for food and service to a reliable caterer. It is the modern way of mastering a large-size reception when you are entertaining at home, or even at a club or hotel, where the maître d'hôtel will take over.

You'll find that an experienced caterer is a real joy to work with in planning your reception. He'll advise you on the type of menu appropriate for serving at certain times of day or evening. Then he will buy, prepare and serve the fare. He will usually supply all waiters, chefs, butlers, announcers, etc., and all equipment needed. If it's a garden wedding, this indispensable man supplies a marquee with canopy, complete with tables, service, beverage and food, plus a floor for dancing. He will even furnish the orchestra, favors and accessories for the wedding, such as rice and rose petals, if you wish. He is as happy to service a small wedding as a large one, and you can depend on him to have a knowledge of correct procedure at his fingertips, to help direct receiving-line protocol, the cake-cutting, the toasts and all the small details that are so important in making a wedding reception go off smoothly.

Talk over all your desires with your caterer, and get everything you decide upon confirmed in writing. Then leave the rest to him.

Buffet is the most popular style of serving at a large wedding, with the dining table stretched full-length down the center of the dining room, with plenty of room for waiters and guests to move around it. A lovely white damask or fine lace cloth reaching to the floor is appropriate for the occasion, with silver candelabra and a handsome floral centerpiece. The bride's cake is sometimes placed in the center of the buffet table, but experience has shown that it is easier for the bridal pair to manage the cutting of the cake when it is either on the bride's table or on an individual table of its own. It should be in a place that can be easily spotlighted for all to see when the cake-cutting ceremony takes place.

If you feel that your wedding is too small to justify the expense of a professional caterer, there is always the private individual in the area who serves at dinner parties and could be engaged to take over, with the help of several assistants. But every detail should be well planned in advance and a dress-rehearsal staged before the big day, so that you can be sure there will be no mistakes. The main concern is that your mother should be completely free of kitchen responsibilities during the entire reception. She shouldn't have to keep one eye fixed on the pantry door as she stands in the receiving line greeting her guests.

It's up to you, of course, to decide on the general procedure for this party of all parties. Here are some suggestions to help you familiarize yourself with reception tradition and the fare that goes with it.

A WEDDING BREAKFAST OR SUPPER

1. It may be a general sit-down breakfast or supper where all the guests are seated at small tables.

2. Or you may have a stand-up affair where the guests serve themselves from a long buffet table while the bridal party only is seated at the bridal table.

3. It may take the form of a stand-up affair served buffet-style to everyone, with no special table for the bridal party.

FOR THE AFTERNOON WEDDING

Small sandwiches and canapés are usual for the afternoon reception. They may be served with guests either standing or seated, depending upon the menu.

Most frequently it is a stand-up reception with the punch bowl as the main attraction for the younger set.

THE BRIDE'S CAKE

The bride's cake should be a beautiful masterpiece. It may be a fabulous spun-sugar confection with tier upon tier and topped with a pair of graceful white doves, an ornate wedding bell or any special decoration you want to dream up. An arrangement of delicate white flowers (lilies of the valley, staphanotis, baby orchids) would make an effective cake decoration when placed in a small glass of water and embedded in the top layer of the cake.

The bride's cake may be a single-tier formed in the shape of a wedding ring. It may even be two wedding-bell cakes, side by side, with calla lilies between them on the table.

Modern pastry chefs are as clever as *couturiers* in designing and concocting masterpieces, so plan for an exquisite bride's cake to highlight your reception table.

Do you know the real difference between the bride's cake and the wedding cake? There seems to be a great deal of confusion about which is which.

The bride's cake is the confection we've been discussing, which is cut and eaten at the wedding. Often it's the only cake in view, while the traditional wedding cake (or groom's cake) is an extra "luxury cake," which may be dispensed with if you wish. It is a dark fruit cake which is usually cut in advance, boxed, and given to guests as mementos to take home.

It is customary for the wedding cake to be sliced and packed in small white or silver boxes, tied with ribbon, which are placed at each corner of the table for a seated breakfast or reception. If you have a buffet affair, the boxes are stacked on silver platters and left on the main table, or put on a table near the door so that each departing guest may help himself. You may buy the boxes already filled at your confectioner's and be saved the bother of doing it at home if time is at a premium.

Here's a way that the bride's cake and the groom's cake could be combined into one. The top tier of the bride's white cake (frosted and decorated just like the other tiers) conceals a tin box, tightly sealed and filled with wedding fruit cake. The lower tiers of the bride's cake are cut and served at the reception, and the tin box saved to be opened in celebration of your first wedding anniversary.

If it's a military wedding, the bride's cake might be baked in the shape of the bridegroom's corps insignia. An impressive white castle as a reproduction of the Engineer Corps insignia, for instance, would be thrilling.

Cutting the Cake

A silver cake knife, festive with a white satin or tulle bow, is provided for cutting the bride's cake.

In an afternoon reception, where the cake is not reserved for the dessert course, you will want to cut it as soon as all your guests have been received. The bridegroom and your attendants will go to the dining room with you and everyone will gather round.

You should cut the first slice of cake (from the bottom tier) and divide it with the bridegroom as evidence that you are willing to share with him now and forever. Usually a servant or caterer's assistant then takes over the cutting and serving of the remainder of the cake. Or at a buffet, the guests may cut it themselves or you may appoint a friend to take on this task.

If your dining-room space is limited and few people can be accommodated, it would be an ingenious touch to have the cake carried to you in the living room, where most of the guests are assembled.

If it is a military wedding, the bride (assisted by the bridegroom) cuts the cake with his sword. She makes only the initial cut (the first piece) and is supposed to make a wish.

BRIDAL-TABLE SEATING ARRANGEMENTS

If your reception or breakfast includes only a few guests, you will all be seated at one table (unless it is buffet-style, of course). You will want to use place cards for everyone, and the seating plan follows:

This same arrangement is suggested for your bridal dinner preceding the rehearsal. It is not necessary on this occasion to include the minister and his wife, unless they are close personal friends. As at any formal dinner, husbands and wives are separated at the table. If you are planning an informal buffet rehearsal dinner before or after rehearsal, dispense with the place-card idea.

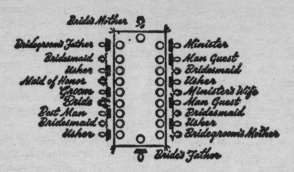

The wedding party will be seated at a separate table if the reception is quite large. Your mother and father, the bridegroom's parents, the minister and his wife, and close relatives should be seated at another table, and your guests will sit where they like at other small tables. If the tables are supplied by your caterer, they will probably be the small round kind like the tables in French restaurants. Or you may use card tables supplied by friends and neighbors.

The bride's cake will form the centerpiece for your table, to be ready at hand when the time comes to cut it. If your bridal attendants are married, their husbands and wives should be invited to the reception, but are not seated at the bridal table unless they are members of the bridal party.

Here is a chart to use as a guide in arranging your place cards for the bridal-party table:

WHAT TO DRINK?

Champagne is the classic wedding beverage. There are excellent domestic brands that are less expensive than imports. If you are having a great many guests, you may have to compromise on a punch of some sort. White wine or a rum punch is often used. A fruit punch, ice-cold and not too sweet, is delicious and, of course, pleasantly mild if it is a hot, thirsty day.

There are many good recipes for nonalcoholic punches. Or you might like to serve the sparkling white grape juice which simulates champagne in taste and effervescence.

Put the punch bowl on a table all its own, out of the line of regular traffic to the buffet table. Decorate it with a great bunch of frosted grapes hanging over the side.

A TOAST TO THE BRIDE

After the cake is cut and the drinks served, the best man usually proposes a toast. He may say, simply, as he stands and raises his glass, "Here's health and happiness to the loveliest of brides."

All in the group, except the bride, then rise, raise their glasses and drink the toast. If the toast is dedicated to both bride and groom, both remain seated. Then the groom replies with thanks for both of them.

Other members of the wedding party and the bride's and groom's fathers may, in turn, propose a toast to the bridal pair, and it may well be a gay, spontaneous interlude in reception festivities. Anyone wittily inspired to propose an original and personalized wish—in keeping with the dignity of the occasion—may do so, but longwinded speeches are definitely out of order on such an occasion.

Following are some simple suggestions on the subject of wedding toasts:

"To the health of the bride and groom—and may they always be as joyous as this wine and as constant as these good wishes, which are eternal."

"Here's orchids to the bride,
    Champagne to the groom,
    Happiness to their union
    And a lifelong honeymoon."

If there are congratulatory telegrams from absent friends or members of the family, they may be read at this time by whoever is acting as impromptu toastmaster.

Usually, at an Army wedding, there is a toast to the bride, welcoming her into the Army. Following this, the best man and the ushers draw their sabers together at the commands "Draw" and "Saber," and cross them to form an arch over the bride's head. The glasses are held in the left hand and the toast is generally concluded with "How!" But don't get so enthralled with this colorful performance that you forget and drink a toast to yourself. You of course remain seated.

DANCING PROCEDURE

If there is to be dancing at the reception, it could properly start right after the best man has given his toast. It is thought by some that the dancing should not start until the wedding repast is finished, but you may start the dancing whenever you wish.

The "traditional" dances always start with you and your bridegroom alone on the dance floor. The drums will sound off, and you will know it's time to take the spotlight.

Following the "traditional" dance custom, your father claims the second dance with you, and your husband asks your mother for the honor of having this second dance with her. The third is danced with your new father-in-law, while your groom takes his mother for a whirl. After that the best man cuts in on you for his dance, the bridegroom asks the maid or matron of honor to dance, then the bridesmaids, and back again to the bride who has been dancing with the ushers. After that the men guests may feel free to ask the bride to dance.

It is agreed that the guests do not go out on the dance floor until the full sequence of the three first traditional dances is completed.

There's another arrangement that is considered appropriate in the dancing procedure. This permits the best man to cut in on the bride and groom after the completion of their first dance, so that the bride's and groom's fathers might ask their own wives to dance their first dance together. The ushers would then cut in on both sets of parents, so that the fathers would be free to follow out the traditional dances with the bride, then claim dances with each other's wives. Whatever the order, it should be for the best man and the fathers to dance with the bride before any guests break in.

The musicians should start to play before the receiving line breaks up.

A BORROWED EUROPEAN CUSTOM

For adding charm and romance to the occasion the revival of an old French custom—the *coupe de mariage* —will delight the heart of any bride.

The custom, as it is practiced in France, centers around a two-handled silver cup of delicate shape upon which are engraved the names of the bride and the groom and the place and date of the wedding ceremony. This small cup may be bought at any good jeweler's, and handed on to future generations for use at their weddings.

The cup, filled with wine, is presented to the bridal couple, and each drinks in turn to seal their troth to a secure, happy and abiding marriage, while all the guests gather around to witness the sentimental ceremony.

The cup may be given a place of honor near the cake, on a little pedestal wreathed with flowers and greenery. The best man may officiate at the ceremony, calling for the guests' attention before the bridal pair shares the cup.

MENU SUGGESTIONS

Even though your guests may have an eye on the refreshments as well as on your wedding gown, don't serve too much. The spirit of the party is the main thing, and sustenance secondary.

Climates and seasons should influence you in deciding on your breakfast or supper menus. A wedding in Virginia, for instance, conjures up thoughts of juicy, succulent ham, while out-of-town guests at a New Orleans breakfast will be delighted to find French or Creole dishes.

Chicken is popular anywhere, at any time. Caterers admit that nothing more appropriate has been devised for wedding fare. So, if chicken it is to be, make it a proud, tempting dish. Cooked in white wine with a clove of garlic, then added to sautéed mushrooms and cream sauce, and served in puff paste patty shells, it is perfect for a stand-up buffet.

Try chicken paprika or chicken in pieces with lemon and sour cream. Substitute fresh green salad for the usual green peas; or baked zucchini, broccoli or wild rice.

For dessert, ice cream is the wedding favorite. Or an ice (but not if the weather is scorching, as it melts rapidly), and always the delicious bride's cake. Then a demitasse, black and steaming.

Sit-Down Breakfast Suggestions

Chicken salad (or chicken patties)
Lattice potatoes
Hot biscuits and marmalade
Mint ice cream   Bride's cake
Bonbons   Demitasse

*   *   *

Creamed sweetbreads and mushrooms
Avocado salad
Melba toast   Chocolate Parfait
Bride's cake
Mints   Demitasse

*   *   *

Consommé royale
Chicken Tetrazzini
Small French rolls
Ice cream
Bride's cake
Mints   Demitasse

Buffet Breakfast

Sliced smoked turkey   Mousse of chicken
Tomato aspic salad   Celery   Olives
Croissants
Vanilla ice cream with brandied cherry sauce
Bride's cake
Coffee   Mints

Afternoon Reception

Assorted tea sandwiches
Lobster salad
Champagne punch

Bride's cake
Coffee and tea

* * *

Ice cream in molds
Bride's cake
Nuts, mints and bonbons
Coffee and tea

Evening Supper

Fresh fruit supreme
Green turtle soup
Rock Cornish hen   Wild rice
Endive salad   Cheese straws
Orange water ice
Bride's cake
Chocolate-covered mints
Demitasse

TOSSING YOUR BOUQUET

Linger as long as you can with your guests after the refreshments. Then throw your wedding train over your arm, gather up your bridal bouquet, and let some of your attendants spread the word around that you are on your way to change. If your bouquet is centered with a going-away corsage, your maid of honor should see that it is placed with your traveling clothes. Toss your bouquet as you start to go upstairs, and may the next bride win!

SAYING YOUR FAREWELLS

When it's time to leave, say your farewells gaily and quickly, but first a few fond words privately with both sets of parents . . . and a big thank-you to your father and mother for making *your* day so perfect. Give family and friends a few moments to wave you off in a flurry of rose petals and cheers.

Above all, don't forget to send telegrams to your parents and his when you reach your honeymoon destination.

As a final gesture, your mother might send you and your bridegroom off in the honeymoon car with the makings of an intimate wedding feast. Tucked in a wicker basket there could be a bottle of champagne, plus opener and glasses, hors d'oeuvres, nuts, mints and slices of bride's cake and its decoration.

CHECK LIST FOR ANY RECEPTION

1. Consider the convenience to guests of the wedding reception locale, parking facilities and the size of the place in relation to number of guests expected.

2. Remember that the reception is the real fillip of the momentous occasion—and plan it with gaiety in mind.

3. Arrange reception acceptances and regrets in separate files so that the number of guests to prepare for is easily ascertained.

4. Don't forget to inform your caterer of the approximate number of guests expected, at least two days before wedding.

5. Decide in advance of the reception just how you wish the receiving line made up (whether the bride's father will stand in line or mix with guests), then inform the bride's parents, etc.

6. If you are going to have an announcer at the head of the receiving line, arrange for him in plenty of time.

7. Be sure to have a suitable knife for cutting the cake.

8. Be sure to remain in the receiving line until all guests have been greeted.

9. Make certain that the minister and his wife are provided with transportation to the reception, and that they are assigned places at the parents' table if you are having one.

10. Be sure to have a guest book for everyone to sign. Usually the best man takes charge of this duty, and may stand near the end of the receiving line, to catch everyone as they go through the line. Or he may take it around to the tables during the refreshment hour. If the best man has his hands full, the maid of honor could be delegated to do this.

11. Remember not to light a cigarette or smoke one while wearing your bridal veil. It is highly flammable, you know.

12. Arrange a signal on timing with your orchestra leader so that the first dance with your new husband will be just right to have the proper fanfare.

13. Remind your bridegroom that he should be ready to respond to the best man's toasts.

14. Have your maid of honor remove your corsage from the bridal bouquet and place it with your going-away outfit, lest you forget it.

15. Make a ceremony of tossing your bouquet while everyone gathers round.

16. Stay as happy as you are!

CHAPTER 13 | Recording the Proceedings

Some society editors like to publish the announcement of a wedding-to-be several weeks in advance of the occasion, then follow up with the descriptive account immediately after the wedding has taken place.

In sending data to the papers, the same rules of good taste should be followed as in sending engagement announcements. Many papers have printed forms that may be filled in and returned to the society department. All proper names should be given in full, either complete first name or two initials. It's a wise idea to take notes as you go along to make sure you have full names of the minister, organist, soloist, etc., as a last-minute timesaver.

It is the bride's family's responsibility to see that the wedding notices are sent to the newspapers at the right time. All accounts should be typed, double-spaced, and addressed in care of the Society Editor. A release date should be indicated at the top of the first page, with the bride's telephone number for verification.

The actual wedding story should never appear in the

paper before the wedding takes place. If the wedding is
held in the morning or at noon, the afternoon papers
would carry the notice first; or if the ceremony takes
place in the evening, the morning papers would get the
break.

TYPICAL WEDDING ANNOUNCEMENT

If there is to be a brief announcement story in advance of the wedding, such a news item might read:

The marriage of Miss Nancy Ann Claridge, daughter
of Mr. and Mrs. Douglas Randolph Claridge of Irvington, and Mr. Lee Cayton Bell, son of Dr. and Mrs. Jo-
seph Lincoln Bell of Chicago, Illinois, is to take place
Thursday afternoon, the fifth of September, in Trinity
Church. A reception will follow the ceremony at Spring
Dale Country Club.

The bride's sister, Mrs. Donald Ross Kerrington of
Boston, Massachusetts, will serve as matron of honor.
The bridesmaids will be Miss Helen Thurman and Miss
Betty Beale of Cleveland, Ohio, and Mrs. George Alden
and Mrs. Wilbur T. Vanness of Irvington.

Martin Hale of Chicago, Illinois, will act as best man
and ushers will include William Wright, L. Roger
Chandler, Jaspar Ingle and Landon Carrington.

The wedding story, which often includes a great deal
of detail—the decorations, costume descriptions, prominent guests, etc.—most likely will be requested by your
local newspaper. Oftentimes the information is given on
the telephone, but for accuracy it is preferable that it be
typed and sent to the society editors.

Your own local papers will be your guide, so follow
their requests. Do have your information well organized
before attempting to give it out. Give full names of all
participants, where and by whom the ceremony is to be
performed. Get the correct names of the flowers from
the florist; have your out-of-town guest list ready for
quotation, etc.

When you wish to have your wedding picture included with the story, you may send in a glossy print, or the society editor may request one. Do not be surprised, however, if the photograph does not run at the time the article appears, for often there is not sufficient space for running both and the picture appears later. The photographer often services the newspapers with glossies, free of charge, if his credit line is used. In some towns the newspapers will send photographers to cover your wedding.

Be sure to keep clippings of your wedding account for your book of memories, to record that day of days.

The announcement of a very informal ceremony simply states:

Miss Isabelle Black, daughter of Mr. and Mrs. Edward L. Black of Dayton, Ohio, was married to Mr. Roscoe Walton, son of Mr. and Mrs. Roy Donaldson Walton of Chattanooga, Tennessee, on Saturday afternoon, the twentieth of April, at the Wesley Heights Chapel, Dayton, Ohio.

A formal announcement of your marriage may be made by your parents if you have married away from home in a very quiet ceremony, thus: "Mr. and Mrs. Walter Huntington announce the marriage of their daughter," etc.

When the bride's parents are divorced, if the bride's mother has remarried and wishes to include her former husband, the announcement in the newspapers should read, "The daughter of Mrs. Thaddeus Burns of this city and Mr. Jasper Chittenden of Baltimore, Maryland . . ."

If, for personal reasons, the bride's mother wishes to omit the name of her former husband, only her name would appear in the announcement, *i.e.* "daughter of Mrs. Thaddeus Burns of this city," etc.

The wedding account of a second marriage rarely includes many details, though the announcements follow the same form as for any first marriage, with names of parents given, etc. The prefix *Mrs.* is customarily used for the bride, *i.e.* "The marriage of Mrs. Alice Lynn Blair and Mr. Felix Wharton Young took place . . . etc."

If the bride's mother (or the bridegroom's mother) is a widow, the following phrasing is customary, "the daughter of Mrs. Oliver Seldon and the late Mr. Seldon."

YOUR WEDDING PHOTOGRAPHS

You will doubtless want to have your posed formal wedding photographs made as soon as your bridal gown is ready. Pictures may be taken at the store where your dress was purchased if there are suitable facilities. When bridal departments are equipped with good photographic studios, the picture-taking operation is greatly simplified. There, veil and gown are freshly pressed for the occasion and much less fuss and bother is attendant than when the bride goes to a photographic studio with all her wedding trappings.

If wedding photographs are taken at home, the simplest sort of background should be used. Often the photographer will provide a backdrop in contrast with your gown.

When the proofs of your pictures are ready, be sure to order glossy prints for the newspaper wedding accounts.

And what about candid pictures? No bridal scrapbook is complete without candids taken before and after the ceremony. Usually time-exposures (without flash) may be taken from the rear of the edifice, yet the scene is recorded and can go into your wedding scrapbook.

You will surely want pictures of you two, smiling happily as you come out of the church.

At the reception there are many human-interest scenes to be taken, besides the "receiving line" and "cutting-the-cake" shots. There are always special people whom you'll want the cameraman to follow about.

Small nephews eyeing the cake wonderingly—and later munching same, are fun pictures to have. Grandparents glowing with pride over the new Mr. and Mrs., old school friends, little nieces in their ribbons and bows, and the next bride-to-be holding the wedding bouquet she has just caught . . . all these, and more, should be included. So if you want them in your album, make arrangements ahead of time, and you'll never be sorry.

CHAPTER 14 | Procedure for Guests

There are certain traditions and customs which the guest at a wedding will wish to observe, along with the natural niceties and courtesies that make up the everyday social graces. When in doubt as to the correct procedure, let consideration and kindness, tempered with good common sense, lead the way—and you'll rarely go astray on etiquette problems.

YOU ARE INVITED TO A WEDDING

The postman has just put into your hands an exciting white vellum square. It's an engraved invitation to a friend's church wedding with a formal reception card enclosed.

You prepare to answer it in formal style, posthaste, even though the reception invitation does not request a response in so many words. It could have said "R.S.V.P.," "Please Respond," or "The favour of a reply is requested." But even though not indicated on this invitation, you know your wedding etiquette well enough to realize that a formal response is expected in all circumstances when a wedding invitation includes a reception invitation.

If the invitation includes the wedding ceremony only, no formal note of acceptance or regret is necessary unless a pew card is enclosed. In this case, a formal acknowledgment is made, out of deference to the bride's family. An invitation to a home, club or hotel wedding which requests "the pleasure of your company" also requires a formal response.

You'll write your formal response to the invitation in your best handwriting, in the third person, on fine white double-sheet note paper. Space it according to the engraved form and follow the same wording, although it is not necessary to repeat every word of the invitation. (Do not use "informals" or tinted note paper.)

The date and time are repeated to show that they have been correctly noted, but the names of the bride and bridegroom are not repeated.

TYPICAL FORMAL ACCEPTANCE

Mr. and Mrs. Robert Karen Clemson
accept with pleasure
Mr. and Mrs. Donald Lockridge Hogate's
kind invitation
to the wedding reception of their daughter
on Saturday, the twentieth of June
at half after four o'clock
Fifty-four Park Avenue

TYPICAL FORMAL REPLY SENDING REGRETS

Mr. and Mrs. Van Leer Justice
regret that they are unable to accept
Mr. and Mrs. Donald Lockridge Holgate's
kind invitation for
the wedding reception of their daughter
on Saturday, the twentieth of June

REPLIES TO INFORMAL INVITATIONS

Invitations by handwritten notes should be acknowledged in the same intimate style and addressed to the sender of the invitation.

Dear Frances:

Dick and I are delighted to be asked to Janet's wedding on the twelfth of August at Graylyn Chapel. We are planning to be there—and to the reception following—to wish the happy couple all the joy in the world.

Affectionately,
Rosemary

An informal note of regret should give the reason for not being able to attend the wedding. For instance:

Dear Frances:

Bob and I regret so much that we will be away on the twelfth of August, for we have looked forward greatly to this wedding "in the family."

We have reservations on a London-bound plane next Monday and won't return for six weeks.

Please express every good wish to Janet and Jack from us. We hope to see them immediately upon our return.

Affectionately,
Rosemary

UPON RECEIPT OF A WEDDING ANNOUNCEMENT

You should sit right down and write personal notes to both the bride's family and the bridal couple.

An announcement requires neither a gift nor a formal acknowledgment, so writing a personal greeting is little enough to do in return for being remembered by the bride or her groom.

IT'S TIME TO SEND A WEDDING GIFT

When you receive an invitation to a wedding reception following a church ceremony, or to a home, club or hotel wedding, it is obligatory that you send a gift. (If invited only to the wedding ceremony in a large church affair, you are under no obligation to send a gift.)

Send the wedding gift to the bride at her home as soon as possible after receiving the invitation. Enclose your personal engraved card and have the gift-wrapped present sent from the store where it was purchased.

If you are married and have no "Mr. and Mrs." visiting cards handy, it is perfectly permissible to write *Mr. and* in front of Mrs. X. If you feel so disposed, you may write a personal wish for happiness to the bridal pair at the top of the card, though this is not usual unless the guest is a most intimate friend of the bride.

Often a business acquaintance of the bride's father, or of the bridegroom, wishes to send a wedding gift to the bride even though she (the bride) has never met the donor. The card, in such an instance, usually includes the name of both the businessman and his wife.

In making your gift selection, it is advisable either to confer with the bride or someone in her family as to her wants and needs; or to seek the assistance of the bridal counselor who has her gift-preference list. As has been pointed out earlier in this book, most altar-bound girls list their silver, china and glass patterns at their leading local stores so that guests may easily obtain such information.

Thoughtful friends do not mark occasional silver articles like candelabra, trays, bowls and odd pieces of flat silver, because of the possibility of duplicates.

When a present is not sent until after the wedding because of unavoidable circumstances, a note should be enclosed, or sent separately, explaining the reason for delay.

SHOWER GIFTS

Unlike wedding gifts, shower remembrances are usually given in person to the bride at party time.

In some communities shower gifts often take the place of wedding gifts. In other communities wedding presents are sent in accordance with the conventions of etiquette regardless of how many showers a guest may have attended. The customs of one's own community should serve as the guide.

CHURCH WEDDINGS

Your arrival as a guest at a church wedding should be scheduled at least a half hour before ceremony time. If it's quite a large affair, you would do well to make your appearance three-quarters of an hour ahead of time.

Guests with reserved seat space should arrive about fifteen minutes before the ceremony. None should be later than five minutes before the hour scheduled.

When guests do arrive late, they should go directly to the gallery and seat themselves, or remain in the rear of the church during the ceremony.

When you enter the church, you will be met at the aisle entrance by an usher who will ask (if no pew card is presented to him) whether you are a friend of the bride or the groom. If you are a friend of both the bride and groom you should so indicate, and the usher will then seat you in the best unoccupied place, either on the bride's side (the left side of the church) or the groom's side (the right side).

A woman guest takes the proffered right arm of the usher and is escorted up the aisle. If she is attended by a man, he walks behind them. A low-voiced conversation may take place between the ushers and guests as they proceed along the aisle.

Feminine guests customarily keep outer wraps, hats and gloves on throughout the ceremony.

Guests should conform as nearly as possible to church rules, as observed by its members, when attending weddings in churches not of their own faith. They should take their tips on procedure from the families in the front pews, but they should not try to carry out church rituals with which they are not familiar.

Though there may be no aisle ribbons to prevent the guests from rising and taking leave after the recessional, it is only common courtesy that all should remain in their respective pews until the ushers have escorted the two bridal families to the vestibule of the church. This includes grandmothers, aunts and all family relatives seated in front pews.

GUEST INFORMATION FOR A HOME OR CLUB WEDDING

Ten to twenty minutes before the ceremony hour is the correct arrival time for guests at a home or club wedding.

The right side of the room, facing the altar, is for the groom's friends and relatives; the left side, for the bride's, just as in a church wedding.

Guests should take their places on either side and remain standing during the entire proceedings, unless chairs are provided for special persons not able to stand for such a length of time.

Women guests do not remove their hats or gloves. The latter are left on until refreshment time.

Guests may chat with those about them until the triumphal note of the wedding march sounds. Then there should be hushed silence.

RECEIVING-LINE PROCEDURE

As guests pass along the receiving line, shaking hands with everyone, pleasant and brief remarks about the wedding are in order. A bride is wished happiness, and a groom is congratulated.

It's a time-honored custom that relatives and intimate

friends are privileged to kiss both the bride and the groom on the wedding occasion.

When the bride thanks her friends for their gifts, as each passes along the receiving line, gracious acknowledgment of the thanks should be made, but no long dissertations or explanations about the gifts should be made by the guest. "I'm so happy you like it," or a brief explanation, "I didn't have it monogrammed so that you may exchange it if there is a duplication!"—will suffice.

DINING-ROOM ETIQUETTE

If the reception is in the form of a large seated breakfast or supper, guests who are not seated at honor tables with place cards may seat themselves wherever they like.

At a stand-up type of party they are served, or serve themselves at a buffet, and move about as they choose. As soon as the bride and groom enter the dining room to cut the cake, everyone gathers around to watch.

After leaving the dining room or the receiving line, guests usually go to see the wedding gifts if they are on display in another part of the house.

After the bride has tossed her bouquet, guests assemble in the hallway or outside the house to await the honeymoon getaway.

Guests should take their leave soon after the bridal couple has made an exit, unless invited to stay for special festivities to follow. In the strict sense of the word, farewells are not necessary at a wedding party, but complimentary words about the wedding and the bridal pair are always appreciated by the bride's family, and are fitting as a guest's responsibility to the party.

SPECIAL NICETIES

If the wedding reception is scheduled to be over at an early evening hour, it is a thoughtful gesture for relatives or close friends of the bride's family to plan an intimate little dinner or gathering of some sort in honor of the bride's family, so that the evening may not suffer an untimely letdown. Wedding aftermaths may be as gala as the receptions themselves, and will fill in the gap for the bridegroom's family and all visiting bridal party members who linger on.

CHAPTER 15 | For Better or for Worse

You as the leading lady of this eventful occasion will, of course, rehearse with all the other members of the wedding party. No longer does a bride have a stand-in for the rehearsal, as was the custom in other times.

For the sake of an absolutely perfect wedding, do practice your own starring role.

WHO IS TO TAKE CHARGE?

Perhaps you've arranged with your bridal counselor to be at the church (or your home) for the rehearsal. If so, she will aid you in corralling everyone and putting each in his place. If not, the clergyman and the organist may be depended on to take charge of details.

There's always an unquenchable spirit of fun at the wedding rehearsal (a cover-up for last-minute nervousness, no doubt), but it shouldn't be too lively. See to it that everyone understands his responsibilities and knows exactly what to do.

Regardless of who is to be in charge of your rehearsal, work out your own ideas with your mother beforehand. Know the procedure you wish to follow and talk it over with your clergyman to be sure that it conforms with his regulations.

You have been working toward this ceremonial climax—your wedding—for months. Give some thought to all the possibilities of pageantry which will dramatize the moment and make a beautiful wedding picture.

WHO SHOULD ATTEND THE WEDDING REHEARSAL?

Every member of the wedding party, including the bride's father, of course.

The clergyman (or clergymen, if there are two) who will perform the ceremony.

The organist.

The vocalists who are to participate.

The bride's family and the groom's family usually are present for a review of the performance.

If your rehearsal follows the bridal dinner, all the guests may be invited to witness the proceedings if you care to have them.

CORRECT PROCEDURE TO THE ALTAR

It is most important that the wedding party have uniformity and smoothness of motion as they proceed down the aisle.

A short natural step is recommended, with no hesitation or sliding of the foot. It should be in perfect rhythm with the music, and the organist will give you the key to the right tempo. Everyone should start off on the left foot and stay in step all the way.

An equal distance must be kept between members of the bridal party as they walk down the aisle. The ushers should have at least the distance of two full steps between them. The bridesmaids and maid of honor should be about eight feet apart, unless the church aisle is exceedingly long and you wish to space them farther apart. There should be about twelve feet between you and the maid of honor (or flower girl).

The procession usually goes down the aisle in the following order:

Ushers (usually walk in pairs, the shortest leading)

Bridesmaids (may walk singly, or in pairs, according to height)

Maid or matron of honor

Ring bearer

Flower girl

Bride on her father's right arm.

The ushers, bridesmaids and all the bride's attendants and her father should take their places in the vestibule. The bridegroom and best man are with the clergyman in the vestry.

Immediately after the fanfare (the first two triumphant bars of the *Lohengrin* "Bridal Chorus") the clergyman enters from the vestry door. The bridegroom and the best man wait until he has reached his place in the chancel. Then the bridegroom enters from the vestry, followed by the best man. (They should not walk together.)

The bridegroom takes his position immediately in front of the first pew on the right, where his family is seated. He half turns so that he may see his bride as she comes down the aisle. The best man takes his place in line with the bridegroom and a pace to the right.

At the same time the bridegroom leaves the vestry, the ushers start their slow tread down the aisle from the back of the church. It is awkward to leave the bridegroom and best man waiting too long a time at the altar, if the church aisle is very long. The groom and best man should be in their respective positions only a few seconds before the ushers reach the chancel.

Following the ushers, the bridesmaids walk down the aisle; then the maid or matron of honor, who walks alone. If you are having both a maid and a matron of honor, they may be dressed alike and walk together, or their gowns may contrast if each walks alone. The one whose title is purely honorary precedes the actual witness, who will stand by you at the altar.

The ring bearer (if you are having one) may walk alone, next, or he may accompany the flower girl, who directly precedes you on your father's right arm.

In a church with no middle aisle, the bridal party should enter by the left aisle and leave by the right.

As each pair in the bridal processional reaches the chancel rail, they separate. Ushers who are on the right side of the aisle take places on the right side of the chancel, turning slightly toward the center. Those on the left do likewise on the left side of the chancel.

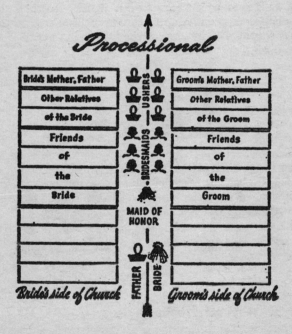

In the same fashion, bridesmaids separate at the chancel rail, taking positions in front of the ushers on each side.

AT THE ALTAR

All attendants stand in oblique positions, half facing the congregation, with their eyes on the approaching bride.

The maid of honor stands opposite the best man. When the bride reaches the head of the aisle where the bridegroom is waiting, she releases her hand from her father's arm, takes a step ahead of her father and stands by the bridegroom on the left. The bride's father remains standing just behind and a little to the left of the bride until he responds to the question, "Who giveth this woman to be married to this man?" He then answers, "I do," and takes his place in the first pew on the left of the middle aisle, beside the bride's mother.

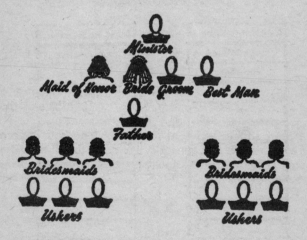

The minister will instruct you in the service, according to his own preferences.

THE RECESSIONAL

The recessional is the reverse of the processional. The bride and groom walk first (bride on her husband's right arm), then the flower girl, the maid of honor on the right arm of the best man, and the bridesmaids each on the right arm of an usher.

You may wish to have the best man retire to the vestry, and the bridesmaids go back up the aisle together, two by two, followed by the ushers. If there is an uneven number of bridesmaids and ushers, this procedure is advisable.

The recessional is a trifle faster in tempo than the march down the aisle, but it should not look hurried or rushed.

There is no recessional in a home or club wedding. The couple turns after the ceremony to receive congratulations of both sets of parents. The receiving line is then formed and other guests come, in turn, to greet the newlyweds.

INSTRUCTIONS TO THE USHERS

The left side of the church is reserved for the relatives and friends of the bride. The right side is reserved for the groom's relatives and friends.

If the church has no center aisle, but has pews in the center, the dividing line extends down the middle of the center pew.

Ushers should arrive at the church one hour before the ceremony. If flowers are delivered to the church, the sexton should see that the ushers receive their boutonnieres.

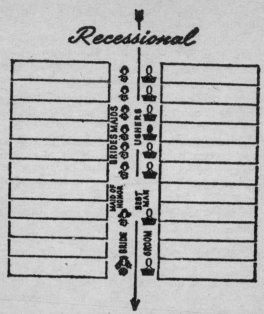

Recessional

An usher, or ushers, should be delegated to stand at each inner doorway leading from the vestibule (or rooms where guests will enter).

Ushers should inquire about special pew cards issued to important guests. They should receive instructions as to seating arrangements for special relatives of each family.

An usher asks each woman guest where she would prefer to sit, or whether she is a friend of the bride or of the bridegroom. He then offers her his left arm and escorts her to whichever side of the church she has specified. They may talk quietly as they proceed down the aisle.

A man is never ushered to his seat. If he is with a lady, he walks a pace behind the usher and his companion.

The usher should pause for a moment at the end of the pew while guests whom he has escorted take their places. He should then return to the vestibule doorway to resume his duties.

About five minutes before time for the ceremony the bridegroom's mother is escorted to her place in the first pew on the right side. The bridegroom's father follows a pace behind and takes his place beside her.

About two minutes before the ceremony hour, the bride's mother is escorted to her place in the first pew on the left.

Special arrangements should be made at rehearsal to delegate certain ushers for the duties of escorting the mothers.

No one is seated by an usher after the bride's mother takes her place.

If aisle ribbons are used, two ushers walk to the front of the church, where ribbons are attached on the front pews, and draw them over the tops of the pews all the way to the back of the church.

The aisle canvas (if it has not already been tacked down by the florist) should be brought from the front of the church to the back by the two other ushers as soon as the first two have returned from drawing the ribbons. The canvas will have been folded accordion fashion when made ready. Each usher holds the outside corner of the canvas strip, and they walk back up the aisle drawing it behind them as they go.

The head usher should arrange for the sexton to give the signal to the organist when the procession is ready to start.

The ushers line up for the procession (in the vestibule) in front of the bride and her party.

Immediately after the recessional, as soon as the bridal party has reached the back of the church, the usher who escorted the bride's mother to her place before the ceremony turns directly around and goes down the aisle to escort her back again. The bride's father follows behind.

As soon as they have reached the rear of the church, the usher for the bridegroom's mother does likewise.

Immediately after both sets of parents have reached

the rear of the church, the two ushers who stretched the ribbons start from the back of the church to wind the ribbons. The guests then are free to leave the pews.

This completes the ushers' duties, and they join the bridal party in the waiting cars to go on to the reception.

At the reception, the ushers (though not in the receiving line) may stand together at one side of the line to speak to guests.

They should mingle with the guests, see that everyone has an opportunity to speak to the bridal party and that no guest is neglected and everyone has a good time.

REMINDERS FOR THE BEST MAN

The best man should lend constant moral support to the bridegroom. After he helps him pack for his trip, he sees that the luggage is stowed in the car for the honeymoon, and helps him dress for the wedding.

He sees that the bridegroom arrives with him at the church a half hour before the ceremony. He takes the bridegroom's hat and coat to the vestibule and leaves them in care of the sexton before the ceremony. He never takes part in the processional, but may in the recessional. He pays the clergyman (the groom, of course, having provided the fee).

He carries the wedding ring to the altar (he may carry a duplicate in another pocket) and presents it at the right time.

He rushes back to the vestry after the ceremony and collects his own hat and gloves.

He calls the cars for the bridal party, proposes a toast to the bride at the reception, sees that everything is taken care of for the honeymoon getaway, and helps the bridegroom change into his traveling clothes.

MAID OF HONOR

The maid of honor will receive instructions from the minister as to the timing of her duties at the altar. She should take your bouquet early in the ceremony; assist you in putting back your face veil just before the bridegroom kisses you; return your flowers to you after the kiss, and arrange your train as you turn to go up the aisle in the recessional.

CHAPTER 16 | "I Pledge Thee My Troth"

Let's suppose today's the day.

You'll wake up in the morning with love in the air and a sparkle in your eyes.

You'll want to laugh and cry . . . and shout and whisper, all at the same time. You'll wonder if this is you . . . you who are going to be serene and calm, come what may. Then you'll tell yourself there's nothing to be panicky about. Mother may lose her gloves, the best man may drop the ring, and the ice cream may turn out to be soup. But you'll take it in your stride and count it all part of the fun.

If you're really wise, you'll linger on and have breakfast in bed. You'll look around and remember that there's really nothing to do. Your going-away outfit is pressed and all ready, with accessories near by. Your bags are packed, except for the last-minute crushables. Your fingernail polish looks benignly pale and correct. And you remember with a start that now is a good time to transfer your engagement ring to your right hand to remain till the ceremony is over and your wedding ring is in place.

Then you'll check on your "list," with a smug little feeling that all those weeks of work are now paying dividends. The out-of-town guests have all been happily quartered. The traffic policeman is scheduled to be on duty at the church. The caterer has moved into the kitchen. You can hear the florist and his helpers in the rooms below.

You have something *old* (Mother's lace hankie), lots that's *new*, something *borrowed* (the bridegroom's mother's brooch), and a new satin garter that's *blue*. Then, there's a shiny dime to tuck in your shoe. Your new white wrap to wear over the wedding gown, orange-blossom perfume to spray on your hair, and your luggage keys in their secret hiding place just in case there are any pranksters about.

You'll start reviewing your gifts and their donors so you can say "thank you" and *mean* it as your friends go through the receiving line.

You'll look back and see in kaleidoscopic review that an amazing number of things have been accomplished and that you *must* be a genius to have pulled together all the loose ends.

You'll think, with a start, that it will soon be time for music and people . . . and all you've been hoping for come true.

You know you'll be smiling and radiant as you walk down the aisle. You're sure that no one was ever so happy. And most of all, you know it's not *just* for today.